The Power of Positive Imagination

Yaya Sillah

ALSO BY THE AUTHOR

Marriage & Society

How to Build the Gambia
(Attaining Economic Super-power Status in Africa)

Copyright © 2017 Suba Kunda Publishing

http://www.subakunda.com

subakunda@yahoo.com

+2209459540

All rights reserved

ISBN: 978-0-646-98053-9

CONTENTS

	Introduction	1
	Acknowledgements	3
1	The power of positive imagination	5
2	Four reasons why you cannot fail to succeed	38
3	The importance of role models in society	108
4	My mentor	147
5	Fear is your number one enemy	159
	About the Author	170

INTRODUCTION

All the praises due to Allah; peace be upon on our holy prophet Muhammad.

On Saturday 29th April 2017, when I launched my book "How to Build the Gambia" at Alliance Franco Gambia Kairaba Avenue, I noticed that all the speakers, including me, struggled to get the attention of children in the audience, and I wondered why this was. I asked myself: are we using the wrong topics to engage the children? Are children lacking motivation to engage with adults? Perhaps they were pre-occupied, thinking only of toys and computer games, or missing their friends who were playing football. How many of those children were thinking about becoming like me when they grow up?

I felt that there was a need to create something which would be equally appealing to both adults and children. The idea of this book "The Power of Positive Imagination" was born there and then. This book would sound like thunder, with flashes of lightning which would strike the hearts and minds of all readers.

In this book I will take a journey with readers to explore ideas and share stories which will mesmerise adults and capture the imagination of children. I will try as much as I can to give my own examples and use my own words. For example, rather than using the old fashioned phrase "blood is thicker than water" I will use my own saying "feeling is more powerful than touching" because feeling is the work of imagination and it has no boundaries. However, touching is the work of emotion.. it's limited in reach.

In the following chapters, I will challenge readers to train their own minds as much as possible so that they might create their own phrases, and come up with their own theories about the world. I am also going to challenge some existing theories related to certain subjects.

At my book launch, in two areas of my speech I challenged Gambian writers "Don't just write for Gambia, but write to get the attention of the international community. Your story is as relevant to them as their story is relevant to you". That has resonated more effectively with Gambian writers than anything else I wrote. Additionally, in the same speech, I challenged my audience to "write the story of your experience, because no one can express your story more effectively than you can. We can learn so much from each other and we can show each other our strength and support each other in our weakness." That statement captured the imagination of people in the gathering more than any other part of the speech. I got feedback from my audience, and I realised that sometimes challenging people that you are trying to engage is more effective than praising them.

As someone with a keen interest in sociology, in this book I will attempt to come up with my own theories. I will challenge contemporary theories and misconceived views held by modern society. However, all my arguments will be purely based on intellectual argument, not just arguing for argument's sake. I am giving an opportunity to readers to come up with their own ideas, so that we can learn from each other. As I stated in many of my previous writings, when someone expresses their opinion, he or she is giving an opportunity for other to express theirs too. There is no point in having an intellect if you cannot use it to create your own opinion, whether you are an intellectual or not.

ACKNOWLEDGEMENTS

As a person who keeps on trying to achieve something better in life, a support network of people in society is essential in attaining any meaningful progress. I would like to give a special thanks to all those who supported me through thick and thin to launch the books "Marriage and Society" and "How to Build the Gambia", the most memorable moments of my life, as well as helping me to make them a success. It's impossible to give the names of every single individual who participated to give me such wonderful support, including the dignitaries who honour my invitation. However, I must make a special mention to Mr. Hassoum Cessay, a historian from the Gambian National Centre for Arts and Culture. Hassoum and his team, including Lamin Yarbo, have contributed much to make the book launching a great event.

Additionally, I would like to extend the same gratitude to my chief guest of honour, Hon. Halifa Sallah, NAM for Serekunda. Halifa delivered an inspirational speech to the gathering. I thank the Hon. D.A. Jawo, the Gambian Minister of Information, who expressed his admiration to the audience. I appreciate the efforts of Mr. Bakary Sanyang at the Gambia National Library and my friend who chaired the ceremony, Alh Batura Jabbi Gassama, the C.E.O of Future Generation Foundation, and Mr. Momodou Sabally at the Sabally Leadership Academy. Ustas Lamin Jammeh, the P.R.O at the Back to School Foundation was instrumental in entertaining the gathering.

Finally, a massive thanks goes to my entire family, particularly my wives and children; as I always say "My strength is my family, without them nothing is possible". In order for me to continue writing, I stole family time to create the space which made it possible to complete two books quickly. After my book launched, the overwhelming support which I gathered from the public, and especially my immediate family and close friends around the world, has strengthened my little brain to imagine even better than before. As a result, "The Power of Positive Imagination" is born.

Thanks also go to Keith and his team in Auckland, New Zealand, who always help me with editing and publishing my books.

1: THE POWER OF POSITIVE IMAGINATION

Traditionally, we believe that human beings have only five senses: sight, hearing, taste, smell and touch. However, I would like to name two more, to bring the total to seven. I would add imagination and consciousness.

1: If you make a careful observation, you can argue that imagination is not a result of the work of the five common senses. It's a sense on its own. My argument is based on the following: disabled people such as the deaf, the blind, and those who are paralyzed from the top of their bodies down to the legs have the ability to imagine things, like any other person. Based on that, I consider imagination as a sense on its own.

2: Consciousness is also a sense on its own. When we go to sleep most of our senses cease operation until we wake up again. However, because of our consciousness, we have dreams while sleeping. After seeing beautiful things in our dream, when we wake up, we use our imagination to remember those dreams and we translate each dream to reality. This unique human ability makes consciousness its own sense.

For argument's sake, you can ignore what I say and stick with the old fashion concept of five senses. Yet, to strengthen my position, I would bring the following to your attention. We used to believe in the existence of nine planets in the universe. But with new discoveries in space, there is no question of the existence of other planets, many more than the original nine. In my opinion, it's just a matter of time before biologists discover more amazing senses in humans, and many more than five.

Until then, use YOUR imagination and accept my theory of seven senses, embark on your own journey and make your own discoveries.

All knowledge started from a single seed of one person's powerful imagination, similar to reproduction of human beings, when a single tiny sperm which from nothing, becomes something massive and unique. You might be a child reading this book wondering "how could my imagination create something as amazing as a human being?" Here is your answer: your most favourite toy, which you always use to play with, is the product of someone who used to be a child like you. One day, he or she used the power of imagination to come up with an idea which would excite children like you and the idea of that amazing toy was born.

By the way, don't under estimate a child's imagination; it's as powerful as adult imagination. Certain were invented by children and children are still inventing many useful objects, particularly in the area of art and design.

Before you proceed to the next paragraph, I would like to bring one of my own quotes to your attention - "Being an intelligent person is not a process of physical strength, it's a process of emotional strength."

As a child, if I ask you, who is the most intelligent scientist? Perhaps you might answer: Albert Einstein. Again if I ask you who is the most intelligent economist? There is no doubt Adam Smith would be your answer. And who is the most intelligent inventor? You wouldn't hesitate to tell me Bill Gates. Now let me tell you how each of them managed to become great gentlemen.

Do you remember Einstein's famous quote "Imagination is more important than knowledge"? Mr. Einstein was exactly like you, a human being, and living day by day hoping that the next day coming is going to be much better than the previous day gone. However, he felt that, making the next day better than the previous one would not be possible without his own contribution. Thus each day he used his imagination to make that possible.

It's extremely important to note that the power of your imagination will determine your own story. It's essential to bear in mind not to measure your success against that of Einstein; let it happen by itself naturally. You have to come to the realisation that every imagination has its own direction as well as its own story. In my latest observation I came to realise that being a great person doesn't mean solely being a wealthy person, it means being more productive in what you do. In order for history to compare you to great men such as Einstein, don't just imagine things; be more productive in your imagination.

Adam Smith took the power of his imagination and built his ideas around it. As a result his ideas are the basis of economic philosophy. Let me tell you the technique he used to achieve that: Mr Smith learnt from the power of other people's imaginations, until he felt it was time to capitalise on his own thoughts. As a result he succeeded in producing the first modern work of economics, The Wealth of Nations.

My theory of success is that it is a continuous journey, travelled by those who want to attain individual goals, set by a person who is determined to control his or her own destiny, without fear of being judged by others or anticipating failure. Adam Smith understood this theory through the power of imagination, and he became his own story.

It's very common for some people to think they are bad at

doing certain things and they wish they could be lucky and become more productive.

Listen to me: it's wrong to think that way, and you are already lucky. Guess the secret of success - it's nothing other than the power of imagination.

Think just for a second: for a man, a single drop of sperm produced is enough to impregnate a woman. If you are a woman, a single egg produced is enough to conceive a child. Equally, one single moment of positive imagination will spark your intelligence and lead you to succeed.

I am a firm believer that every human being is productive in one way or another, but sometimes the late discovery of your talent is the obstacle to your progress. Because of this, I would recommend you create a special time and space which will allow you to use the power of your imagination to produce something meaningful, not just for yourself but for the whole of humankind, so that one day, you will be as celebrated as Albert Einstein or Adam Smith. Powerful thinkers didn't just become influential individuals by accident; they made a powerful mind through the power of their imagination.

By reading and believing in religious texts, we often convince ourselves that our destiny is not always in our hands. I think that approach is not helpful to modern society. The recent great advances such as Google, Facebook, the internet and so forth were all the products of great minds inspired by the power of imagination. Don't think for second that I am borrowing my ideas from an atheist school of thought. My position of monotheism is very firm and it's not going to change. However, I am willing to confront some of the baseless ideas which are causing our society to drift into anarchy.

Among those ideas are those of the lazy individuals who still hold the old fashioned view that they don't have to think for themselves because God is going to provide everything for humankind here on this planet. This may be the truth but in my opinion God has provided everything by giving the human beings a fantastic mind, with the amazing ability to think and produce their own power of imagination. You might be a very religious person like me, yet my opinion on religion is this - the intention of religion is to humble the behaviour of mankind, and it gives hope particularly during the period of grief, sadness and misery of death whenever it arises. Being religious doesn't mean you have to hate yourself or hate others who don't hold your beliefs.

The important of using the creative mind from a religious perspective

From ancient times, the prophets used their imagination long before they received any divine revelation from God. According to the holy Quran, the prophet Abraham (Ibrahim) did exactly that. When he was a child, he used his imagination to make sense of the world around him. Ibrahim initially refused to accept the gods and goddesses of his people. From the beginning, he pointed his finger to the shining star which mesmerised him, and he adopted that star as his God for a while. He would subsequently change his mind and adopt the moon as his God, but through effectively using the power of his imagination, he eventually chose the sun to become his God. The more he used his imagination, the more he learnt the reality of, and became aware of, his environment. When it became apparent to him all those celestial objects were not God, finally God inspired Ibrahim to know the truth, because Ibrahim used his imagination.

It's narrated from Muslim tradition that in the sixth

century, before Muhammad became a prophet, he isolated himself from society in Arabia for six months to meditate in a cave near the Jabal an-Noor mountain, outside the Holy City of Mecca. During this period, Muhammad followed the example of Ibrahim by depending on his imagination to make sense of the world as well as contemplating the meaning of life, and what happens in the afterlife.

As a result God chose Muhammad as his messenger and prophet. God knew Muhammad was the right person to disseminate his message to human beings.

Meditation by using one's imagination is recommended by Islam. Encouraging people to think and use their own mind without relying on others helps them use the power of their imagination, which is more effective for psychological reconstruction and building society than any other tool. You might have thought otherwise but this is the Holy Grail of intelligence. It's not only important in the creation of a productive society, but it's also important for your personal physical wellbeing.

From a Christian point of view, meditation using one's imagination is commonly practiced within the church and the home. Most Christians believe this inspired the production of the holy gospel.

Do you now realise that the miraculous power behind the imagination is unlimited? Would you be shocked if I tell you that Steve Jobs, the inventor of the Apple brand, used his imagination to create such a world class communication system which was beyond any human perception? The Apple brand became the darling of the 21st century and Mr. Jobs gained the reputation of having one of the most powerful minds ever. Genius doesn't become genius by accident; it is the fruit born by the power of imagination.

Before we proceed to the next paragraph, excuse me for one second but I would like to interrupt your reading just for five minutes. Together, let's practice how to use the power of imagination. Can you please you leave a mark here to ensure you don't lose your place? After the exercise I am about to give you, we can resume our discussion.

Wherever you are right now, make sure there is no noise which might distract you from this crucial moment. Sit comfortably, facing the direction where the sunshine comes to you in the morning; and try to relax your body, just like you do when you try to have afternoon nap. You don't have to close your eyes, but you can, if you feel sleepy. Breathe in and out slowly while you imagine trying to connect with the image of Steve Jobs, Albert Einstein or an inspirational person like them. From the start, you will struggle to focus and concentrate properly to connect with anything useful. And at the same time your mind may wander while your brain is trying to make sense of your ambition, but within the space of five minutes your mind will mirror that of the inspirational person you chose. Through the power of your imagination you are embarking on a journey and spiritually travelling to reach a destination which is beyond that inspirational person's achievements. Repeat this practice as much as you can by following this example at least once every day - eventually you will be able to connect with the power of your imagination which will determine your future.

I have recommended this method for some people in the past, and so far the benefit is so good for them. Throughout this book, I will demonstrate different ways to maximise the power of your imagination.

Please don't confuse this form of meditation with worship

of someone or something other than God. By meditating this way, you are not replacing the practice of your daily duty of worshipping God. Spiritual growth as well as social growth isn't possible without having inspiration from someone or something through meditation.

Religious fanatics who are opposed to any form of human advancement and independent thought might discourage you from undertaking these essential steps, but they are very important to your personal intellectual growth and human spiritual advancement.

While doing my own research as to why some countries are more advanced and developed than others, I reached the following conclusion: poor and disadvantaged societies are societies full of stagnated minds, and as a result poverty is pandemic. Social exploitation is always a common occurrence in any society where people are not equipped to think for themselves. For instance, if I can use Africa and South Asia as examples: they are victims of stagnated minds, exacerbated by a lack of interest in using the power of their imagination. Their communities are totally relying on others, particularly Europeans and Arabs, to think for them; consequently their societies are massively handicapped - intellectually, medically, socially, and economically.

In my view, the advancement of one individual person in a remote corner of Africa and the advancement of one backward society in the highlands of South Asia is equally crucial to the advancement of the world in general. Human advancement isn't limited to certain geographical locations. However, the slow pace of increasing public awareness of the importance of an open-minded society hampers intellectual progress in many countries. What people have to understand, particularly people in Africa, is this: being an open-minded person, means being a person who is prepared to accommodate more ideas. The more ideas a person has the more opportunity is waiting for them. The human advancement we see in Europe, USA, Australia, and elsewhere is a result of an open-minded society which makes personal growth possible. Personal growth subsequently leads to community growth, through individuals using the power of their imagination.

My book captured the imagination of the customs officers in the airport

Let me share this very interesting story with you. There is a saying "You cannot judge a book by the cover". However, the title of a book can capture people's imagination before they read it. I will give you a flavour of how the power of imagination works sometimes.

On Saturday 29th April 2017, on the very day of my book launching, at around 11am I went to the UPS international carrier to collect the parcels containing the copies of my book "How to build the Gambia". On my arrival at their service centre, located not far from Westfield Junction in Serrekunda, I was told by one of their agents that three boxes of books had been seized by the Gambia customs department at Yundum international airport. According to the agent, custom officials seized the parcels because they claimed such large quantities of books were for commercial purposes. As result I had to collect them and pay any tax required by the Gambian revenue authorities.

Straight away, I went to the airport. I followed the normal procedures by obtaining a clearance form from the customs service and completing it. When I submitted the form, one customs officer was chosen to accompany me and examine the parcels before they could determine what was to happen.

When he opened the parcels, the book's title "How to Build the Gambia: attaining economic super-power status in Africa" immediately captured his imagination and he said "Wow, that's a very interesting book. Who wrote it?" I told him: the name on the cover, Yaya Sillah, is me. From using my imagination, I could tell from his facial expression that he was very delighted with my work. Then the officer took five books as an example, to show his boss, as required by customs law, and I accompanied him. When we reached the boss's office, the customs officer presented the books to him. Again the title of the book captured the imagination of the boss, exactly how it did to the junior officer earlier on. His exact remarks to me were "The title of your book is very interesting, Mr Sillah; it has captured my imagination and it's a wakeup call which will definitely trigger Gambians to debate how to build our country."

And then he added "Mr Sillah, I am going to waive the duty from your books. You are not going to pay a single dalasi. In addition, you will not pay any additional customs handling fees because you are contributing immensely to national development, particularly in the area of intellectual improvements. Therefore on behalf of the managing director and the entire staff of the Gambian civil aviation authorities, waiving the duty is our contribution to your book launch and is in recognition of your efforts."

Hearing those wonderful remarks at the airport on the day of my book launch, I wanted to make a gesture of thanks so I went to the store, opened the parcels and I distributed a copy of my book to each customs officer present that day and personally autographed each one, and added the words "God bless you", which became my trademark. The power of imagination in one sentence had worked: it was as if I had I cast a magic spell on the innocent custom officers at the airport.

It wasn't the content of the book which mesmerised the customs officials: they had not even read it yet. It was the title of the book which had captured their imagination. My primary goal was to share my opinion on how to build the Gambia, and I sparked a debate right there at the airport, simply by choosing a powerful title for the book.

From this experience, you can see one spectacular aspect of the power of my imagination. This is how I would like to see your imagination working for you every day. Throughout this book, I will give you many examples including quotes from the world's most powerful thinkers and famous people, each of whom, through the use of their imagination, has conquered the world. Although nothing comes easy without hard work: you cannot achieve something massive without putting effort and dedication into it, but at times that simply means understanding how to use your inner self and reach your full potential. It will cost you nothing, not even a single dollar.

How to enhance the power of your imagination

By now you might be wondering "Yaya, why on earth do you keep bombarding us with talk of the power of imagination without giving us a single drop of information on how to enhance our imagination?" Good. Because you picked up a copy of this book and you've read it up to this stage, there is no doubt in my mind that you are a serious person who wants to know how to use the power of your imagination. I challenged you at the start; you are challenging me now. I am absolutely happy to share my experience gained through my research and understanding of sociology. I will share everything with you.

The following are the most effective tools to enhance your

imagination:

1. Meditation. According to many reliable sources, Steve Jobs, the former Apple CEO, used to meditate at a Buddhist temple in Indiana, USA, before he obtained the full power of his imagination and invented the Apple brand. By performing a daily meditation you are highly likely to reach a level of spirituality which you would not be able to attain without meditation.

2. Music. There is much evidence that, Michael Jackson, the King of Pop, became who he was thanks to the power of his imagination through listening to music. Everyone is different; some people like to listen to music which makes them emotional - through that emotion they attain spiritual growth and enhance the power of their imagination. For some people, any sort of music will do it for them. Whatever works for you, stick with that as long as it takes to fulfil the power of your imagination.

3. Prayers. Religious peoples like me usually rely on prayers to reach the power of imagination. Not only saying a prayer, but prayer mixed with mediation, in a quiet place far from any distractions. For the faithful, prayer is the most fundamental objective which connects them to God. Prayer can also help someone attain the peace of mind which is essential for achieving the power of imagination.

4. Walk with purpose. Whenever you go somewhere on foot, walk with purpose by imagining you are achieving something which is dear to you. This logic may sound too simple and easy, but it's one of the most effective weapons to attain a creative mind.

I would like to repeat the famous quote by Albert Einstein – "Imagination is more important than knowledge". This not a mere opinion of a great thinker, but it's stating a fact.

It captured my imagination. Every now and again in this book, I will bring it to your attention until it captures your imagination.

5. Frequent walks on the beach. Traditionally, water has a mysterious power which has always captured imagination. People sitting by the river bank and couples walking holding hands together on the beach: this is a common pastime for the rich, the powerful and the famous to refresh their minds as well as improve their imagination in order to achieve big things together. Frequent visits to the sea side, particularly in the mornings and evenings, would improve your mind to attain peace and tranquillity.

All that you need to do is this: sit somewhere quiet and comfortable by the river (or sea) and look straight in to the beauty of natural water without blinking your eyes too much. You will eventually feel that your mind begin to rest and it will focus at one place on the water. Concentrate all your attention on that particular place in the water and its beauty, which will erase the burden of stress from your mind, and develop your creative mind through the power of imagination.

There are many other techniques you can use, but for now we have to test our understanding of what we have already learnt and put it to good use.

I have stated already that all knowledge began from someone's imagination. You probably already have all that it takes to create your own knowledge. But you should also remember this - curiosity is the foundation to all knowledge. Being more curious leads you to ask more questions. The more questions you ask, the more answers you get and the more knowledgeable you become.

We must use our intelligence to create our own success. As

human beings, we are all an intelligent species; however, we are not all talented enough to show our intelligence to others.

In the next few pages before we turn to the next chapter, I would like to demonstrate how you can convert the knowledge you gained from the power of your imagination into action.

Act on your imagination

Do you believe in the saying "Actions speak louder than words", because I don't! Does that sound crazy?

Here is my alternative concept - "Actions are more productive than words". Do you see my point? Do you remember that I said I would keep on challenging you? I am challenging you to come up with your own theory about whether actions speak louder than words or actions are more productive than words.

If you use your imagination, you will create your own knowledge. You don't have to keep on clinging to other people's opinions and old fashioned irrelevant sayings. Don't get me wrong; it's absolutely okay to learn from others as much as you can, but relying on your own intelligence is more effective than anything else.

As you can see, I use other people's ideas and their quotes. But the more I write, the more I create my own knowledge. Do you remember David Cameron's famous phrase "You can do anything if you put your mind to it." I don't believe that. I believe that you won't achieve anything if you fail to use your imagination. Who is right; David Cameron or me? Just use your imagination and drop me an email and let me know what you think.

One night while meditating on my prayer mat, I wondered why snakes don't travel in groups. Whenever you see a snake he or she is always alone; what is the logic behind that? To answer this question, you don't need the intervention of an animal expert: create your own knowledge and come up with a brilliant answer. In 2014, while resting on the top floor of a house somewhere in the world, I saw a plane flying high in the sky. I wondered would I notice on the ground if the aeroplane experienced turbulence in the sky? If not, why not? Don't ask an aviation expert, just drill a little hole into your brain, reach for the power of your imagination, and create the knowledge of the millennium.

Bill Gates did that to create the mighty Microsoft computer empire. Here's his take on success:

Have energy, don't have a bad influence. Work hard, create the future, and enjoy what you do. Play bridge, pick good people, and don't procrastinate. Have a sense of humour and ask for advice whenever it's necessary.

I am not going to attempt to argue with him on these points. He makes a fantastic observation. The way you approach life is fundamental to your own success, as well as helping others to attain success. If you'd had the success that Bill Gates has had, I am sure by now, you would believe you could achieve anything if you put your mind to it. But lack of action will prevent you every time from accomplishing your dreams. You can read as many books as possible to generate more ideas, or enrol yourself in colleges and universities around the world and keep furthering your education, yet without acting on what you learn, trust me, you are just wasting your time.

A graduate of Cambridge University in the UK and a secondary school dropout in a remote village of Africa are all equal by essence. The only difference between them is who is more willing to apply the power of their imagination and take action.

Let's use this story as an example

I know of someone who was out of work and had to depend on social welfare for survival. However, she refused to be defeated by hopelessness; and she acted on her ability as a great thinker and produced something amazing from the power of her imagination.

Guess who that person is? JK Rowling, the author of the Harry Potter books. She used the power of her imagination to create those stories. They then captured the imagination of the international community, particularly children and young adults. Within a short period of time, she gained the attention of people in every corner of the globe. By using the power of her intelligence, she accomplished a unique achievement: for the first time in world history, overnight, books made an author a millionaire.

Do you want be like JK Rowling? Of course you can be! Here comes her advice:

Take action on your ideas. Failure helps you discover yourself. You will be criticized, so remember where you started, and believe in what you do. There is always trepidation. Life is not a check list of achievement. Persevere: dreams can happen, we have the power to imagine better.

While you digest this wonderful guidance, take a break before we use what we have already learned.

What we have learned so far

Often when we wake up, we feel fresh and optimistic for the dawn of a new day, that feeling of turning the page from the miseries of days past and contempt towards people who we blamed for causing our failure.

However, a proactive person, who has ambition to accomplish his or her dream, embraces every new day with resilience. Nothing will stop them from becoming who they really want to be. Every day, with confidence, they use the power of their imagination to achieve their dream.

You can be that person. Here is how to begin, but before I tell you, I want you to realise this fact - self-discipline and having confidence in yourself is the key to the door of success.

The first thing you need to do when you wake up in the morning: wash yourself and brush your teeth. If you are a religious person, do your morning prayers as required by your faith and when you finish prayers, go and greet your spouse, your parents if they live with you, and your neighbours. If you are not fasting, have a small breakfast, after which, relax just for few minutes before embarking on any journey. Use the power of your intuition and map out where you're going today, what you will do when you get there and what your plans are for the rest of the day. Just for a moment before you leave the house, do a little meditation. While meditating, visualize the kind of success you are yearning for. When you finish, put on smart clothes, head to the door and embrace the fresh air just for a second before you embark on this important journey. And every day before you step out of the door, please store the next small paragraph in your memory.

Always bear in mind that our fear of failure when trying something new is exactly what brings failure upon us. Consequently for most people, fear is the main obstacle to progress. Remembering this is the fruit for my own little success so far.

When you leave your walk in a straight line on the side of the road or on the footpath. Don't look down on the floor like a hungry midnight dog looking for a dinner. Hold your head high, without showing rude pride or envy at anyone. Don't keep your hands in your pockets like a frustrated school boy in the wintertime and don't feel shy like a western stranger walking in the quiet streets of Kabul in Afghanistan. Whenever you talk to people, look them straight in the eye and show excitement like someone who has just won a ten million dollar contract. Walk with purpose, while imagining success in whatever you are pursuing. Until you reach that destination, constantly follow your heart with all your ambition. Slowly but surely, one day that ambition will conquer the world.

By the way just a small extra piece of advice; in many cultures, it's always helpful if you engage people as you pass by, by extending greetings to them. You don't necessarily have to be too selfish by only focusing on you and your success.

Nowadays, it's very common for everyone to carry using something like headphones to entertain themselves while jogging, for example. But the best tool to keep your ambition alive is to keep yourself far away from any potential distraction which may obstruct your mind from thinking clearly. The way you conduct yourself on the street helps you visualize your ambition through using the power of your imagination properly, in order for you to put it into action in the future.

It's extremely important for you to observe all your surroundings, particularly the tall buildings. Imagine owning a massive skyscraper, and one of those luxurious vehicles going up and down the street. Being conscious of your surroundings is not only essential to improve your ability to visualize your achievement, but it's important for your own personal safety.

Whenever I read books related to success and goal-setting, I notice errors made by the authors. They mainly tend to focus too much on issues affecting people, rather than encouraging people to change their attitude on how they approach the challenges facing them every day. Some authors are too busy criticising society; they pay very little attention to the psychological aspects of their readers.

In my view, most of the time, individuals in our societies don't usually put enough effort in to solving their own problems. It's very easy for us to keep on blaming our failure on government, on organisations, on our family members, on God and so on.

Here is my take to tackle the issues of laziness: will it take a rocket scientist to convince you that nothing comes easy in life? Whatever you want to achieve will only come through your own hard work, dedication and passion about making your own dreams come true. There is a concept that a person will only become successful, or world-class, after investing ten thousand hours of effort into doing so.

In most countries around the world, whether developed or developing, nowadays unemployment is always skyrocketing. Yet how many of us wake up every day and are prepared to go out there and look for jobs? How many of us ever try to keep on revisiting our minds and creating something unique? Creative thinking would surely help us to find work and maybe build a company, using the power of imagination.

Human beings are all created equal. Our difference comes

in the way we evaluate ourselves socially and economically. The problems which confront society now had previously confronted society in the past. Yet, hard work and community resilience rescued people from catastrophe. Society has always functioned by facing inconveniences such as lack of employment, lack of suitable medical care for all, lack of essential community services, lack of quality education for children, lack of communication facilities, lack of affordable housing and so on. They will always continue to be our problems. But if each individual in society is willing to properly look after their own economic affairs, poverty and the unnecessary financial stress engulfing communities would dramatically reduce.

It's unfortunate for brilliant minds that are depending on the social welfare system for their survival, and receiving donation from charities, particularly in Europe and the USA during the recent surge of unemployment. I realised that often if one person fails in the society eventually the community spirit to strive for meaningful economic progress also slowly collapses. On the other hand, frequently when a single person succeeds economically, the whole community will strive to emulate that person which is why individual economic achievement is absolutely relevant to the advancement of each society.

Human beings are all superior beings, created equally by God. There is no such thing as inferior; you only become inferior if you believe that concept exists. Consequently it's never too late to rectify manageable mistakes. Most people lack the stamina to use their natural talent produced by the power of imagination, as they have got used to being perceived as inferior by the class system. This backward culture hinders economic growth in many societies.

Basically, from that culture's point of view, these potentially brilliant minds don't contribute anything useful to society. Such an attitude is still common in Africa, South Asia, the Middle East and Eastern Europe, where there is still the concept of 'the elite are the intellectuals'. As a result minds which could produce creative ideas are controlled by certain groups. Consequently just handfuls of individuals intellectually prosper. Academic freedom and independent intellectual thinking is still in its infancy. Those considered to be inferior, and those who are outcasts, have very little choice in using the power of their imagination and taking action to produce something meaningful for society. Side effects of this backward culture include continuous severe economic impoverishment, constant starvation and intellectual stagnation.

The difference between human beings and animals is as follows: human beings are governed by their common sense as well as guided by their will power. Animals have neither. As a human being, if you deny your common sense and use of will power, surely you would live equal to animals.

In order to make sense of what am trying to say; let me quickly bring the following statement to your attention - every human being is a potential criminal, yet each individual's moral strength and fear of humiliation is what guides them to do the right things. If each person couldn't express his or her imagination and willingness to share the products of their intelligence, they would not be able to claim that they are part and parcel of human society. In order for anybody to be able to function properly as a full human being in society, they have to exercise all their rights, particularly the right to express their opinions. That notion of existence is pretty good for each and every society.

There is no more powerful gift from almighty God which

is more effective and more important than the individual human mind. You don't need permission from anyone else to peacefully express your opinion through using the power of your imagination.

Having confidence in yourself and what you do, with discipline as well as good character, goes a long way towards establishing you as the next key person of influence in the community. Don't let yourself be psychologically defeated and destroyed by negative remarks towards you. Embrace life everyday as if it's the last chance you'll have and there will be no tomorrow. Only with such an attitude will you get reward for your best efforts. Do not feel jealous of other people's success, or envy rich, famous and powerful people. In the past, they all used to be like you and one day you could become like them. Don't let other people pull you down by accepting their negative comments and criticism for no obvious reason. Do your best to encourage your family and friends to tolerate and embrace different ideas and accommodate other people's culture and views. If you want to maintain the position of a key person of influence in society, you must be willing to create boundaries to determine what is acceptable to you from your own religion and culture. It's essential to remember that each culture was created by individual people, usually based on a common interest with collective community responsibilities. However, if the fundamental core values and principles begin to fade away, it's essential for individuals with creative minds to intervene and take responsibility by ensuring that appropriate measures are taken to restore those values.

Most religions are divinely inspired institutions. However, the task of translating religious texts is done by religious scholars, a handful of intellectuals who are familiar with such language and understand how to decode them for faithful. But as I said earlier, human beings are not perfect. There is always a chance of corruption in religion because unscrupulous intellectuals conceal the true meaning of religious text. A handful of unprincipled scholars pursue their own agenda for personal gain or political reasons to help certain group of people in society. It's important to always be careful and use the power of your imagination to double check matters relating to life and death situations, and ideas which may harm national security and/or community's cohesion.

Whether you belong to the fan club of Michel De Nostradame (more commonly known as Nostradamus) or not, one thing is certain; you cannot dispute his ability as one of the most gifted creative thinkers who ever lived. When I first heard about him, his story immediately captured my imagination, because of the following.

1. He not only successfully predicted events many centuries before they occurred, but he even predicted the detail of how, why, when and where they would occur, astonishingly including names of individuals associated with such events.

2. His prophecy is not always favoured by some academics, who sometimes ridicule him for lack of clarity. Also they argue that his prophesies were only learnt about following the occurrence of major world events and not before. They created doubt about the accuracy of his prophecy, but this rarely affected the position of his loyalists, including his die-hard supporters in Europe and the USA.

3. In my view, Nostradamus by all account is a genius of creative thinking, because his prophecy was based on the product of his imagination; for the faithful, you don't need science for proof of prophecy.

The gift of Nostradamus vindicated my long held belief that, no matter what your circumstances are, you should always take advantage of your situation to do something amazing in your life. He faced many challenges in his life, including the loss of his entire family to the great plague of Europe. However, the misery of family death even strengthened his position in becoming a more creative thinker. With a proper mind-set you can use any situation to overcome your misgivings and transform them to knowledge through the power of creative thinking. As David Cameron said "If you put your mind to anything, you can do it." I am going to add there is no especially good time for doing anything. Any time is the perfect time to achieve something amazing. I believe anything is possible in this world through the use of your powerful imagination.

The effect of bad imagination

Constantly I emphasise the use of imagination. For argument's sake, some people might wonder whether any imagination is good imagination. Some may say it is, but if I can borrow your attention just for five minutes, please use the power of your common sense to decide right from wrong. Imagining doing bad things is not productive, neither for you nor society. For you to use the power of your own imagining to harm yourself is all part of imagination isn't it, however, it's not useful to you or to your community.

What I am advocating here all along is this: productive imagination which helps you and your community. That is what I mean - nothing else, period. In order to illustrate my point properly for example: the atomic bomb is the product of bad imagination. It's a weapon which made the world vulnerable to complete annihilation in just a few seconds. I can list many side effects of the consequences of bad imagination, but I will draw your attention only to a handful throughout the book. Other examples of bad imagination include: self-harm or suicide, to contemplate and rape someone, fighting with your family and friends, anti-social behaviour, hating innocent people, intolerance of other people's views and beliefs, and lack of empathy for people's suffering.

The power of prayer with using your imagination

Very often these days you hear people say that there is no point in praying to achieve anything in life. Also it's common to hear people complaining that God is not answering their prayers.

God answers the prayers of every single individual, no matter which religion they belong to. The problem lies in how they usually perform their prayers and their state of mind while they do it.

I think it's absolutely essential for me to share with you some of the interesting techniques from my own spiritual experience, so that you can embark on your own journey, and which would surely help you to reach your destination. But once again, before I do that, you might need to take a break to refresh your mind, in order for you to learn and store what follows.

Basically, I will start with a logical explanation which will be followed by a spiritual journey. But first of all, forget the old-fashioned concept of "you only pray when you feel it's necessary", like taking a loan from a bank or begging to survive during a time of dire need. That's not what prayer is about. Delivering daily prayers is to continue to seek the spiritual blessing which is has been one of the most important fundamental pillars of human existence since the beginning of time. The essence of it is not only confined to receiving reward from God through prayer or gaining worldly goods, but it's a highly significant connection by seeking blessing through divine intervention, which would earn you spiritual favours from all deities, keep your heart humble and bring you closer to almighty God.

Hope and confidence are the two most important secrets which you can use as weapons to prevail whenever difficulties arise. Prayer is the fruit of hope and confidence is the fruit of prayer. Don't think for one second that I am biased in my explanation because I am a religious person. That is not the case. This is based on my social experience, which includes opinion from people I personally consider to be free-thinkers and agnostics.

Often when you read self-help books, the familiar words you find in them are: resilience, empathy, patience, politeness, sacrifice, humour, self-awareness, forgiveness, hope, and confidence. In my view; each of these values is connected to a spiritual dimension in the hearts and minds of each individual person. It's impossible to achieve any of them without softening the heart to accommodate them. It's exactly because of this, I associate each of these sentiments as the fruit born of prayer. When you pray, you open your heart to these values.

Before you start your prayers

Make sure that before you start to pray, in anything other than an emergency situation, that you clean your physical body and your spiritual body, as well as the actual place in which you are conducting your prayers.

This is not only essential for your personal wellbeing but it's important for your spiritual connection to God. According the analyses of clinical psychologists "the condition of the human body and the environment in which you live greatly influences the state of mind, body and soul". Do not ignore this fact: it's 100% the truth.

After cleaning the body and the place to start your prayers, the most difficult aspect of all is this: to clean the mind, heart, and soul. Spiritual cleansing is the most challenging aspect to anyone particularly when the heart and mind are full of doubt and greed.

Everyone fails to attain satisfaction in sexual desire and/or accumulating wealth and glory. Swallow the pride of your ego; conquer your intimate feelings with understanding of this reality. Instead, use your sexual energy to become more productive in arts and creative thinking, and use prayers to strengthen the mind. Perhaps through this, happiness is within your reach.

Activate your intuition to reach the goals you set. While praying, use the power of your imagination to visualise the success you are praying for. Focus all your attention to almighty God as if you are seeing him right in front of you. Make sure there are no distractions around you which may divert your attention. Be sincere in your prayers: it's no joke. Avoid mentioning trivial things in prayers like "I want a baby but I don't want one who cries', "I want to fly in an aeroplane but I don't want there to be turbulence", or "I want a second wife but I don't want my first wife to be jealous". Prayers like that are not relevant, and a waste of time and energy. Seeking anything through prayers must be realistic and genuine. Instead of praying for a baby not to cry, pray for a healthy child; rather than praying for no turbulence during the flight, pray for a safe flight, and instead of praying to prevent your spouses from becoming jealous of each other, pray for peaceful cohabitation.

Using the power of your imagination during prayers and

visualising the success you are aiming for enhances your ability to be a creative thinker. Creative thinking is all about being productive in what you think, as well as willingness to take action on your ideas. A positive body means a positive mind, and a positive mind means a creative thinker. Intoxicating the body with alcohol, drugs, junk food, and tobacco prevents a healthy life style, which is really essential for the mental well-being of a creative thinker. The chemicals which can affect someone physically would most probably affect them spiritually as well. A healthy lifestyle goes a long way towards helping you to achieve your goals.

If you act on the following guidelines, it might help to enhance your ability as a creative thinker.

1. Have enough sleep every day.
2. Eat well without taking too much fat into your body
3. Exercise the physical body regularly, as well as the spiritual body
4. Use incense or perfume during the prayers
5. Preferably, wear light clothes
6. Every day, set time aside for each prayer
7. Don't speak to anyone while praying

By adhering to these rules you will be more focused on setting goals and achieving your ambition. The strength to carry on fighting to become who you really want be is better than losing hope. To spend a significant amount of time praying for success is better than gambling daily and hoping to win the lottery.

Life is all about ambition and aiming to translate your dreams into reality. As the saying goes "dream big, achieve more", Try to remember dreams you had during sleep so that at a later stage, you might use the power of your imagination to realise those dreams. If you seek a solution through prayer you will develop resilience, self-confidence, self-awareness and self-esteem, as well as experiencing frequent good dreams, and lack of stress. Via this experience, the capacity your imagination will be more effective.

In 2016, I conducted research in relation to prayer while using the imagination. The result indicated that people who use the power of their imagination during prayers were twice as happy as those who don't. The significant numbers of people with whom I conducted that research were all from different age groups and family backgrounds. However, people involved in the research all belonged to the Muslim faith. Because of this, some people may dispute the accuracy of my finding.

Now let's highlight the dangers of using imagination negatively particularly if you happen to be a spiritual person.

As human beings you are designed to make mistakes. But you are considered to be a fool if you frequently make mistakes. Don't use the power of your imagination to generate ideas which would cause you to hate certain people who don't share your views or values. Avoid using the power of imagination to bear a grudge against those perceived to be your enemies, and don't be greedy for more wealth, envious of other people's success, jealous of your siblings, or contemptuous of others. Understand that people occupying privileged positions are not your arch-enemies.

Don't look down on people who are not as fortunate as you. It's not wise to use the power of prayers to put a curse on people, or hate the innocent, the weak, and the under-privileged. Please remember that the hate crimes that are devastating the world and causing destruction to human lives and properties are the result of someone using the simple power of their imagination. Also be aware that every magnificent structure existing today is the product of someone's powerful imagination. You have the choice to either work with the forces of good or to work with the forces of evil. I choose to work with the forces of good.

From the power of my imagination, I reached the following conclusion. As human beings, we use our emotion when we get angry. We tend to use our psychology when we get sad. We are always desperate to use our imagination when we get lost and try to find a solution. And we tend to use the three combined whenever we get happy in order to give comfort to ourselves. Such unpredictable behaviour is responsible for all our actions whether they are good or bad, and make it harder for us to think rationally.

We must always strive to use our intelligence in every situation, critical or not critical. In that way we can think better and use the power of our imagination properly. To me, a good person is someone who sincerely expresses his or her own genuine thoughts and bears no grudge against anyone. Base on this notion, we can all practice to strive and use the power of our imagination to become a good person in our own way.

Using the power of your imagination is not only confined to creative thinking. For an example: you can use your imagination to know truth from fiction. I don't want to be too self-referential in this book, however, I cannot resist the temptation not to share these encouraging words with you. When I decided to write my first book "Marriage and Society", I used the power of my imagination to put together the experience which I had gained from my spiritual work in relation to marriage and other important social issues.

I had always dreamed of writing a book, and one day I turned my imagination into action to produce "Marriage and Society". Furthermore, after the 2016 political impasse in the Gambia, I used the power of imagination again to write my second book "How to Build the Gambia", which subsequently led to writing this book. If I can do it this way, surely you can do it too, so that together we can achieve many amazing things in the world. The beauty of using your imagination is it's free of charge for everyone.

I gave a speech to around 400 children at one of the schools receiving sponsorship from my charity, the Back to School Foundation. During the speech, I thought that I had managed to get the attention of almost all the children in the classroom, which is very rare. Yet, it appeared to me that the children were not only concentrating on my speech, but they were so mesmerised by me even though I had never met them before. I could read excitement in their faces. After I finished the speech, I wondered for a few seconds what was going on in their mind. Would they use the power of their imagination, like I do, to become who they really want be? Maybe each of them would become even better than me. Do they ever think now about the importance of imagination? I still wonder that sometimes.

There is a common concept which says that "with high risk comes high reward". Is that true or false? Well, it's true to a degree. But for children in this generation, there is no higher reward than dreaming big to achieve more than your father did. Training your mind from childhood with self-discipline would enable you to become a constructive person with a creative mind. The essence of attaining a creative mind includes distinguishing right information from wrong, with regards to daily news bulletins, books, networking with people, etc.

To the best of my knowledge, all the information in this book is the truth. You can use the power of your imagination to challenge me if you think that's not the case. Just drop me an email, I love to engage in intellectual argument with others. However some people might say that "every other opinion than my own is rubbish". Such attitude is particularly common among those who consider themselves to be very religious people; if you have already subscribed to such a mentality, then bye bye, I am not interesting in engaging with you, unless you are willing to be open-minded.

In this last paragraph of the chapter, I would like to introduce Leonardo Da Vinci, the genius creative thinker. Da Vinci created art works which became blueprints for products which were only built five hundred years later, through the use of imagination. Despite little conventional educational background, Leonardo created things which were so advanced they could only be built much later on
As I am using my imagination to write this book, perhaps there are millions of other people around the world using their imagination to produce something incredible. People who rely on others to think for them are ten times less successful than those who are willing to take action on their imagination and produce their own success. Since you have taken action by picking up a copy of this book and reading this far, I am sure by now that you have generated enough experience to use the power of your imagination.
Finally, apart from mentioning their names and their achievements in using the power of imagination, I didn't attempt to provide more information on other aspects of the lives of people like Bill Gates or Albert Einstein. It might be helpful to you to understand them much better if you do some research to find that out for yourself.

Let's go back quickly to think about seven common senses, rather than five. I think I gave enough explanation to you, which include genuine evidence which backed my argument. Consciousness and imagination are the two most fundamental aspects of the human rationalisation process. Remember that, you cannot rationalise the action of an irrational person, particularly if that person lacks the capacity to understand the value of common sense. No matter what I say in this book, or how well I describe things, there is always a small chance that it may not influence an irrational person. However, I think the book serves as guidance to those who are willing to embrace different ideas in order to enhance the power of their imagination, and become more productive to themselves and society.

2: FOUR REASONS WHY YOU CANNOT FAIL TO SUCCEED

In the end everybody wants to be number one but in the beginning we all want to achieve more than one thing.

If you belong to a sports club and you want to win a medal for your team, how many steps do you have to take in order to achieve your goal? Maybe millions of steps.

In 2014, I was watching the football match between Manchester City and Liverpool on Sky TV. Both football teams have incredibly successful records and experienced players, each of whom was determined to score a goal for their team and become the champions of the Premier League at the end of the season. While receiving huge support from the crowd with massive expectations on the shoulders of each player, everyone was striving to score a goal and become a star like Yaya Touré (my own favourite Premier League star). Even though I am not a football expert, I saw that it was apparent that everyone was working hard with tremendous team spirit, particularly during the second half. During the match, I tried to learn from the game as much as I could. I noticed that every single person playing the game was playing very well, but also trying to enjoy the football as much as possible.

But in the end, like any other game there had to be a winner, which on that occasion was Manchester City, by three goals to one. From that day, my perception of how to succeed was dramatically changed. I realised most people's approach to success wasn't going to work. What does work is this:

1. Team work with team spirit

2. Hard work with patience
3. Have determination to follow the dream and become a star, and
4. Take the right steps to reach the destination

Simply watching this match helped me to build myself socially as well as spiritually and I became who I am now.
I hope you won't be upset with me if I repeat how I define success and what it means to me.

Success is a continuous journey, undertaken by an individual who set out to attain each goal and was determined to control his or her own destiny, without fear of being judged by others, or anticipating failure.

This is not only my opinion but is also fact. You can achieve success if you believe it is attainable through hard work, and not through wishful thinking.

Success is not confined only to monetary gain, which you might show off to your friends by visiting the Egyptian pyramids, or spending a whole month in Disneyland France, or taking your family to Dubai for three weeks holiday. These are not what I consider to be success: they are just the trappings of it.

It's only at the beginning of a journey that a motorist worries about the traffic ahead of them. But as they continue on their journey, they care less about the traffic on the road; in fact they enjoy it when traffic is gradually building on the motorway.. their vision is full of vehicles travelling in different directions, driven by many people at different speeds. In such a situation, they don't feel lonely any more, particularly if they have a good travelling companion; the journey is both simple and easy.

This is the journey of success. While you are trying to be

successful, fear, uncertainty and doubt might constantly play in your mind. Yet at that moment, you're not the only one who is striving to attain success. Every day, millions of people like you embark on the same journey. But what makes a difference is how you plan to take that journey at the start.

If you are travelling by land and decided to use the car, did you check the engine to make sure it's in good condition? If you are travelling by the sea, do you have a good boat, and did you check the weather forecast and sea conditions? You can think of other examples.. an aeroplane, a bicycle, walking.. the choice is yours. Make sure before you set out that your method of travel is a good one, and there are no problems.

Equally in order for you to accomplish a dream, you always need to come up with a plan which would enhance your ability as a confident and disciplined person to succeed. It's essential to have a role model who can serve as a guide to build the road map which will make it easy for you to attain success. Otherwise you are doomed to fail from the start.

Now here is a million dollar question before I continue with this conversation: how long do you want your success to last? And how many times will it be necessary for you to fight to achieve this success? I will try to answer that.

The four reasons why you cannot fail to succeed

1. You are willing to take a chance
2. You are willing to take a risk
3. You are willing to put your ideas into action
4. You are willing to learn from your mistakes

Let's explore reason number one - "You are willing to take

a chance". If you just graduated from university, with a degree in information technology, someone might just offer you a job in the tech industry with very little salary. Maybe you are not very impressed with the job offer because of the low wage. My advice would be to take this first opportunity. It's a chance you can use as a stepping stone. It would help you to develop and enhance your experience, which would surely open the door for you to later embrace many other opportunities, which might include an impressive job with an impressive salary.

Listen to this advice from Richard Branson, the Virgin C.E.O:

Keep it simple and give it a try. Be a leader, don't give up; delegate and treat people well. Shake things up: peoples will be sceptical but affect life positively while you are doing things differently.

For me, I think he hits the nail on the head.

Take a chance on your qualifications

You may be very skilful and intelligent but without taking a chance on your qualification, you won't realise anything. Most people feel comfortable working for others and depending on others. However, building you own business or creating your own company is far more efficient and beneficial than working for other people.

Let's say you are skilful in factory work. Rather than waking up every day, rushing to work, and coming home at the end of day with little reward and little respect from your boss and co-workers, make a business plan to create your own factory. Creating your own company is a journey. You have to check the method of travel and the weather to ensure a smooth and safe journey. Make sure you do research for information which might be relevant to your business, and home work to determine the proper direction for your company. Find a good location for your business, pick good people and a perfect management team, make a better marketing strategy, make sure sufficient funds are available and make sure you maintain a good relationship with competitors.

If you don't have sufficient fund to establish the business, don't hesitate to approach your family, friends, banks or credit companies for a loan. However, taking a reasonable amount of loan is more appropriate. At this early stage, having financial discipline with confidence, strength and trust in your ability is really crucial.

Remember that, it's all about taking a chance. With luck comes success, with bad luck comes failure. A good plan increases the chance to succeed, bad plans or no plans won't. Don't take your first chance on something which other people have tried but failed, but it's worth taking in to account all that you can do differently. While focusing on the new business, be honest with yourself, know your strengths and admit the weak points where you need help. New ventures require people's full attention and concentration so that they might be able to move on to the next step.

To Bill Gates, this is the key:

Have energy, don't have a bad influence, work hard, create the future and enjoy what you do. Pick good people, but don't procrastinate, have a sense of humour and ask for advice whenever it's necessary.

Surely he cannot put it better than this.

What rich and powerful people say is not equivalent to your personal experience. Choosing a role model will give you motivation, particularly if you are a business person.

Model your business on those who excelled by following logic and good business strategy.

I am sure in every community there is no shortage of successful businessmen and women. Invest in the knowledge you have, as well as the expertise you learned from other people, including the experience gained through networking. Maintain a positive atmosphere at work and treat your employees very well. If you remember from the beginning of the chapter, the experience we learnt from the football match between Manchester City and Liverpool - team work and team spirit is the Holy Grail of success.

No matter what, when undertaking a new venture, you will be faced with many challenges, each of which will shake your confidence like wind shakes the leaves on a tree, but in the end you will have the last laugh. In life, nothing comes for free; whatever you aim to achieve, it won't come without sacrifice and hard work.

In saying that, don't let money consume your entire mind like wild fire consumes dry grass. Always remember, in modern society, money is the evil cause of much conflict around the world. Sadly, with no other alternative to replace it, money is too precious to abandon.

Try to predict events before they occur; being a businessman is all about predicting what will happen in the financial market. If you acquire this skill, it won't be long before you establish yourself mentally and emotional to deal with stress, which increases the chance for growth in your business and soon you will be starting to make a massive profit.

Nobody is born with business D.N.A, but with determination and dedication they achieve something which is only a dream to some people. Efficient communication skills help you to maintain a healthy relationship with your customers. Nurture your employees and foster your clients to claim your rightful position in the Richest People list.

Take a chance on what you believe

If you believe you are naturally gifted with technical know-how, take a chance on your belief and become an engineer. Trust your intuition by visualising your dream and turn it into reality. Putting dreams into practice is the mother of all success. From such ideas come Facebook, YouTube, and so on. Those who invented these social media platforms took a chance on what they believed would work and made it work perfectly.

Humans beings are made of different components which genetically harbour unique cells which relate to the discovery of certain knowledge here on earth, thus our body is designed to send a signal to our brain when there is a need for a significant discovery. Automatically this is put to use by those believe they can physically or psychologically reach their inner self. Their intuition visualises a product which they eventually create to become useful materials or objects for society. In order for the person to be able to draw on their mind and create the map to manufacture that product, they need confidence that they have sufficient resources to invent those ideas. It's only then their instincts would kick in to trigger the useful discovery and put it to practice. No one can make you believe it's possible; only you can take action and take your chance on what you believe.

It's common in our society to hear people claim that through faith it's possible to reach your inner self. Through that intuition, you can create something new. If you adhere to that school of thought, taking chance on your belief is very crucial. Don't be afraid; taking a chance is all about trying to put your theory in to practice. Without taking that chance, you won't know whether it would work or not.

There is no guarantee of success in anything; however it is guaranteed that if you don't take a chance, someone else will. I love to take a chance on what I believe, and most of the time it works for me. Just one example: the whole of society would not be prosperous if people didn't take a chance on knowing each other, taking a chance on getting married and having children, and so forth.

One personal example: during 2016, the political crisis in the Gambia after president Jammeh disputed and rejected the election result, led the small African country known as the Smiling Coast of Africa to become the Crying Coast of Africa. In January 2017, the U.S.A and the United Kingdom gave travel advice for their citizens to leave the Gambia with immediate effect due to the imminent threat of war. With such an unprecedented atmosphere, I decided to rush to quickly buy a ticket and return to the UK as soon as possible.

I managed to get a one way ticket and it cost me D29400 - far more expensive than usual to fly out from Yundum to London via Brussels. We were scheduled to fly out on Friday 20th January, just before the end of the deadline set by Ecowas forces for the possible invasion of Gambia, the removal of Jammeh, who was to be replaced by Barrow as President of the Republic.

However, after all that drama when I went home, I sat in my bedroom thinking about what was next for the Gambia? At the same time I tried to make sense of the whole situation by asking myself what, how and who? I contacted a few people I trusted for any ideas on what would happen next but they couldn't give me any satisfactory explanation or respond to my questions. I didn't receive comfort from anyone. So I decided to conduct my own research to gauge the mood of the nation, and particularly the Army, for any possible sign of war. I used the power of my imagination and my political instinct which told me that it was highly likely Jammeh would back off at the last minute to give a chance for peaceful resolution. I decide d not to leave the country, and cancelled my ticket.

I took a chance, and it worked out perfectly. Later on that day, again I went the airport to witness the departure of president Jammeh to exile. The chance I took earlier meant that I knew my own self better and discovered my strength in a crisis, and it opened my eyes on how to deal with a life-threatening situation like that. Please understand that every chance is a potential opportunity, especially if you firmly believe that it's worth taking; and if you do, you will be rewarded.

In the late 1990s, one of my friends wrote an application to a leading university in the U.S.A. to further his education there. His application was successful. They agreed to enrol him to study medicine for four years and sent him an acceptance letter. So he made a student visa application at the US embassy in Banjul to get entry to the U.S.A. A few weeks later he was invited for an interview, during which doubt was raised on my friend's ability to study due to his poor financial background and immediate lack of knowledge of the field of medicine.

Taking all that in to account, the officer said "I don't believe you are a genuine student who wants to further his education. You fail to show evidence of sufficient funds which would enable you to complete your study in the

U.S.A. and you fail to provide proof of any family ties in the Gambia which would demonstrate your intention to return home after the end of your studies. However, I will grant you a four year student visa, which will give you a chance to travel to America and study medicine. But if you fail to return home at the end of your study, the Department of Immigration will track you down and deport you back to the Gambia."

Granting a student visa to my friend enabled him to successfully further his education in America. And it equally gave a chance for many people in the Gambia to use him as their role model and further their education in the US too. The officer's willingness to give a chance to my friend created many opportunities for Gambians who went to study in the U.S.A. My friend did complete his study and returned to the Gambia as a qualified doctor. He became prominent in the Gambian medical system and he is now contributing immensely to the health sector.

It's extremely important for those occupying higher positions to understand that willingness to give a chance to others will cause society to become a centre of peace and harmony, and it could reduce the levels of poverty and crime, and enhance social cohesion. If underprivileged people are not given a chance, there will be no social mobility or opportunities for them.

If underprivileged people are given an opportunity, the government will not have to give them welfare, and those living in the third world countries would be empowered and become more financially independent. I am a firm believer that everyone deserves a chance, not only in relationships, but in other aspects of life.

For example, many people are serving terms in prison, and despite the misery of life behind bars, often with long sentences and hard labour, at some point they can be given the chance to come out and rebuild their lives. In my view, such magnanimous moves from world leaders are a brilliant attitude towards nation building. Yet those who are on the receiving end should embrace that chance seriously by accepting this wonderful gesture from the authorities, and have a willingness to leave their dark past behind and seize the opportunity to become good citizens forever.

On the other hand, from a religious perspective; perhaps you might have committed a great sin in the past and you are now worried of God's punishment for you now or in the hereafter. If you truly believe that it's never too late to receive a second chance via the mercy of God, then you must try and repent before God and ask forgiveness from him. Perhaps after demonstrating such regret, all your sins will be forgiven

Finally, no matter what society you are belong to, or under what circumstance you might find yourself, please do not lose hope. Make sure you strive to take every chance created for you, wherever it comes from, either through the mercy of God or the magnanimous nature of human beings. It's only then you can truly claim that you built yourself to become who you are today.

The second reason why you cannot fail to succeed

People who are willing to take risks are usually more successful than those who don't. From the beginning of the time, mankind conquered the world with knowledge by taking risks to accomplish what it wanted, particularly during times of hardship. It became a tradition for human beings to take a calculated risk whenever it was necessary.

Taking risks is not only confined to life and death

situations, it's much broader than that. It includes taking financial risk, or participating in sports which involve physical risk, or travelling to a dangerous place with the intention of increasing wealth; risk can be taken in many other aspects of human life. For instance, let's use the example of a high school student just graduated in IT. He feels (let's say he though it could be a female too) that maybe there is a need to take a calculated risk and establish his own motor retail business to begin with, yet sufficient funds are not available. Despite all that, he decides to approach the bank for a loan to invest in this new business. Most people might think he is crazy, or too ambitious. The shadow of his lack of experience would cast doubt in many people's minds, and they might think he doesn't have what it takes to create such a company successfully, even if in reality he is capable of doing so.

However, generally speaking, without sufficient funds available and little experience, it is a highly risky move to approach the bank for a loan. But if we look at it another way, for this high school graduate to have the guts to take such calculated risk, that is in itself a brave step in the right direction, particularly if he believes that with higher risk comes higher reward. Saying all that, I would say ideally most people would feel comfortable if his business included someone who had previous experience of running such business, so that the risk could be minimal.

By contrast someone who has capital for investment but lacks the guts or the willingness to take risk due to fear of failure is even worse off. Fear is the main obstacle which prevents most people taking risks, and taking risks is one of the key to success. Risk is a component of success - full stop. Consequently, the heads of large corporation and leading manufacturing companies in large industrialised countries are all big risk takers, which is how they got where they are today.

There is no aspect of human life which does not involve risk. In the beginning of the chapter, the football match I used as example had many elements of risk taking place. Football players risk breaking their legs, hurting their arms, as well as damaging their brain. But despite all that, each striker would strive to play the game with determination and score as many goals as possible. With that intent, success eventually comes their way.

Risk with determination to win is more effective than risk with hope to win; because the latter is just wishful thinking and the former is taking action with responsibility. It's important to point out the different between willingness to take a chance and the willingness to take a risk. The willingness to take a chance comes hand in hand with being too careful not to ruin that chance; however, the willingness to take risk is hand in hand with taking huge responsibility for your actions. But by handling each action properly, it's exactly that which makes a difference.

In the end the risk takers get rewards on the risk they take and those seeking a chance get rewards on their willingness to embrace the chance, although there is more potential for those who embrace both actions together.

The risk of all risks

Just a few centuries back, who would have imagined that one day human beings will fly high in the sky to wherever they like and however they like, without receiving aid from angels and invisible spirits. Such prophecy was only the prediction of one "mad" scientist Leonardo Da Vinci. But such fantasy is now no longer a dream of one man; it's a reality thanks to Da Vinci and others taking risks to accomplish their wild dreams.

The magic behind this comes from the power of someone

using his imagination. They didn't only imagine it, but they acted on their imagination. Without a willingness to take a risk in first place none of those wild dreams would ever have come true. If we look at what it takes to make commercial flying possible, there are five risk factors, each of which is enough to put someone off. The first risk was the high chance of losing money spent to gather the raw materials to assemble the body parts and the engine of the aircraft. Secondly, the chance of explosion of the jet fuel. Third was the risk of flying the aircraft itself, because that was knowledge never put into practice before. Fourth was the risk in marketing the business to earn public trust of aircraft as a mode of transport. Fifth is the risk of not making a profit after the cost of operation and aircraft maintenance. Despite all this the wild dreams became reality.

The point which I illustrated above has vindicated my point that risk without determination is useless. We might be sceptical to give a loan to that graduate student to establish his own business; however, he might be just as successful as those who built the first commercial aircraft. If his determination equals that of the engineers who built the aircraft, surely he would be equally successful. All that he needs to do is make sure he does his homework properly to determine which area of his business is most vulnerable. He should have the honesty to seek help whenever it's necessary to do so, employing a good accountant, and a sufficient amount of workers, and create a good marketing strategy for his business. With such a strong team in hand, defiantly taking a risk with all the right people on board, surely he would excel in this business, maybe within a shorter period of time than most people would imagine.

This is what is known as a calculated risk. Anyone failing to follow this model is doomed to fail.

With my faith, I am willing to take a risk

For the faithful, divine intervention makes anything possible, however, it's essential to use logic and rational thinking in every human situation, particularly when it comes to family affairs. From my own personal experience, I took a risk based on my faith a number of times but each time I did, I made sure I did it with lot of care and responsibility. One such example was on the 8th of July 2005, the day after the city of London was attacked by terrorist suicide bombers (7/7). A few days earlier, I had arranged a business trip to visit one of my clients living in Oldham, near Manchester. On that trip, I was expecting to earn at least £900, however, due to ongoing security concerns in London and its surroundings, the clients I was supposed to visit advised me to postpone my journey to a later date. At that stage I was not desperate to earn money, but on principle I adamantly refused to cancel my trip.

The main risks were copycat strikes by religious fanatics, massive delays affecting the London Underground services, and the high chance of cancellations on the national railway service. The government had given advice against non-essential travel in the country. Despite all that, I took a risk based on my faith that whatever was going to happen to me would happen regardless. Cancelling my journey would have meant that the terrorist had won by putting fear in me. I took the risk. After 10am, I left my house and headed to East Ham tube station where I joined the London Underground District line to Mile End. From there I took the Central line to Tottenham Court Road, then I finally boarded the Northern line to London Euston, where I caught the train to Manchester Piccadilly. At Manchester, I got a bus to Oldham where my client lived with his family. On my arrival he embraced and hugged me. His family really appreciated my bravery in travelling from London to Manchester on that day. They prepared a nice lunch for me and we ate together in their house. After lunch I conducted my business there until the evening, when I went back to London without facing any difficulty what so ever, in addition to earning much more money than I was bargaining for.

I would like the readers to take the following example from this experience. I took the risk based on my faith but it was a calculated risk. Apart from fear of further terrorist attack and the media speculation which exacerbated government reaction in giving such travel advice, there was no imminent danger to anyone, or any credible threat to human life and property.

On the other hand, if there was a group of terrorists on the loose in the City, or a particular part of London was under siege and I had to cross that area, I wouldn't have risked what I did to put my life in such danger. In those circumstances, it would be extremely important to assess the situation and make sure there was no immediate danger to me and my surroundings.

Let's explore another risky moment which further expanded my horizons: one Friday in June 2007, I left my house in Manor Park. I was on my way to attend my usual Friday prayers at Forest Gate with the Gambian community. As usual, with the London summer afternoon rain pouring everywhere, I was running late to catch the bus in order to make prayers on time. While waiting for the bus on Romford Road opposite Manor Park Library, an attractive medium built Asian man, tall as well as smart with a white Muslim dress and long beard drove by the bus stop, but a few moments later he reversed the vehicle back to me, lowered the driver side window and yelled in my direction "Brother, are you going to the mosque?" I said yes, he asked where and I replied "I am going to Durning Hall Community Centre in Forest Gate where Gambians gather to perform Friday prayer." He invited me to join him in his car, and he would drop me off there.

Without thinking twice I dropped my usual guard and got into the car, and then he accelerated the vehicle to continue the journey towards Forest Gate. While seated in the front passenger seat next to him, wearing my seat belt, I was feeling very nervous with an overwhelming fear of the unknown. However, I noticed he was listening to a holy Quran CD. When I saw that I was more at ease. Immediately, I tried to release the panic and fear which consumed my mind earlier: after all, it was a good atmosphere in the car. I engaged the stranger in conversation as much as I could so that I could get to know him better and make sense of why he decided to give me a free ride from Manor Park, all the way to Forest Gate. During our conversation, I learned he often gave a free ride to people. Definitely the gentleman was a very kind Muslim to develop such good habits. He told me always he did similar favours for people and he vowed to continue to do so. In that risky ride, I was struck by one thing in particular, when he offered to share with me the food he had with him. I thought "What a generous man" and I took comfort from that until he dropped me off and continued with his journey.

On both the above occasions my actions involved taking severe risks, but the first risk was different from the second. The first time I took steps before setting out and time was at my side to calculate the outcome and plan in advance; however, the second time I accepted a free ride from a total stranger without having time to plan ahead or think properly to assess the risk.

But in each of these cases my willingness to take a risk was based on my faith. My religious conviction and the concept "whatever is going to happen would happen no matter what;" reinforced my willingness to take the second risk. I also thought that I am on my way to attend Friday prayers and whatever happens to me, God will be there to look over me.

I think it's important to emphases your willingness to take risk doesn't have to involve matters of life and death, unless it is absolutely necessary, say if someone was threatening to kidnap you, or all of a sudden you were caught up in a terrorist attack, or living in a conflict zone. Usually in such circumstances, maybe there is little time to plan ahead and think clearly. You might have no option but to take a risk in anything which could get you to safety. By contrast, no matter what, don't take a risk in anything which involves taking your own life or the lives of others by thinking that you are doing it for God and he would reward you in paradise after doing so. Such a sick attitude is common in today's society, particularly among unemployed youths living in the metropolitan towns and cities who are influenced by a distorted version of religion. Trust me, endangering the lives of innocent people is wrong under any circumstances and there is no justification whatsoever for such barbaric acts.

People's willingness to take risks may vary based on their cultures. What is considered as a risk in place "A" may not be considered a risk in place "B". For instance, an arranged marriage is considered a significant risk in contemporary European society, but it's normal in contemporary Africa and Asia. Although in modern Africa and Asia the practice is deemed to involve a risk of misunderstanding between families, yet people still risk and practice it and it has worked perfectly for the majority. However, in modern Europe, if you feel it is worth taking the risk of arranged marriage, why not go ahead and try your luck?

All you needs to understand in every situation which involves risk is this; the willingness to take a risk is all about a step into the unknown, particularly when the risk involves material objects such as money, gold, diamonds and property or intellectual properties like a career, emotional love, the power of talent, public fame and manual skills. When taking a risk, in order to minimise the possibility of misfortune, make sure you execute it with good timing, better planning, and if it's necessary, team spirit with team work, hard work with dedication and passion to achieve your dreams.

Common sense would tell you don't take risks while being sick or when you are under the influence of alcohol or drugs, which might cloud your mind from rational thinking. There are times when you don't feel yourself, perhaps due to some personal circumstances or family matters, but in the end those awkward moments slowly fade away with time; whenever you happen to face such moments, that is the time when it is suitable to relax the body from all worldly troubles and focus the mind to remove distractions and try to fill your mind with good memories. Life will always reward you with more than you can ever imagine, especially when you regain your confidence in facing the world.

Some cultures deem it highly risky to marry someone you only just met. However, in some parts of the world, such a practice is common, particularly in rural areas. Because everyone is familiar with each other's culture, just by knowing someone's name you can determine their character, behaviour, manners, perhaps even if illness existed in their families. Those who are living in that kind of environment may think it worth taking the risk to marry. In saying that, any form of social engagement such as relationship, marriage, friendship, and dating are all risky businesses. No matter how long you have known a person, the element of risk is always there. That is mainly due to unrealistic expectations behind lifelong commitments. The presence of those realities should not intimidate you from undertaking such a union. As I said before, most aspects of human life involve risk. There are millions of peoples out there who successfully took risks in their lives by gambling on spending time together, and being rewarded in the end.

Being willing to take a risk usually comes with huge rewards in social matters, especially if it's married with hard work, dedication, passion and team work with team spirit. Perhaps it might not be good idea to take a risk in the following areas: gambling money, a one night stand, inviting strangers to your house, participating in armed robberies, borrowing large amount of cash from unscrupulous lenders, using fake documents like counterfeit certificates, and all involvement in criminal activities which could haunt you in the future. Apart from these, always have a desire to take a risk for your own advancement.

If you are in a leadership position or your authority is above others, you must develop your willingness to take a risk in helping others who are less fortunate than you, particularly when those people are looking for employment. Often the boss who simply says yes makes a real difference in lifting somebody from poverty to a better life. Those filling the posts of company directors, doctors, teachers, police officers, religious leaders, departmental managing directors, government officials and other business people play a significant role in society. Their service often involves a huge risk in helping members of the public who are in dire need of realising their potential.

Company directors often take a risk in employing people who lack experience, in order to give them an opportunity for advancement. The same is true of doctors; they risk infection in examining patients. The willingness to take a risk in these honourable men and makes a significant difference to our society. The ultimate sacrifice frequently made by men and women in uniform with unquestionable willingness to risk their lives to defend the sovereignty of each nation deserved our respect.

It's wise always to measure the risk you are taking and compare it with the benefit you get from taking it. For example, a newly established business owner might risk taking a loan of $10,000. By contrast, an experienced factory owner might risk taking a loan up to $100,000. Each of these business owners would manage their loan based on their experience. More experience mean more chances to make profit from the risk taking and vice versa. But the beauty for both is the willingness to take a risk in first place.

Be willing to take a risk of the unknown

Just a few hundred years ago, many Europeans took an unimaginable risk in their quest to conquer the new world. Such a massive exodus by Europeans migrating to unknown parts was nothing other than the ultimate sacrifice and they risked everything for it. That new world is now known as the United States of America and Canada. A few centuries later, similar steps were taken to conquer other parts of the world, such as Australia, Africa, and Asia and many small islands around the Pacific Ocean. Surely without the ultimate sacrifice from those who took a huge risk, such unimaginable human adventure would not come to pass. However, with their religious conviction, guided by perseverance and resilience, in the end they got their reward.

In the sixteenth century, the willingness of Europeans to make this step into the unknown had nothing to do with their experience. You don't necessarily have to wait until you gain enough experience to take a risk on something which will take you to the unknown. All that it takes to get there is conviction, resilience and emotional strength. With these tools in hand, any time is a good time for you to venture into the unknown. Completing your homework in advance would be useful and make sure you follow your heart wherever it takes you by firmly holding the belief that "no matter what, the best is yet to come for me". If you do this, you will get an amazing reward from the risk you take. Each successful person living in your neighbourhood was once a risk taker; each of them realised that opportunities are always shrouded in mystery. Mystery is the hiding place of success, therefore risk is the mother of success.

Whether you are a student, a teacher, an engineer, or what have you, your willingness to take a risk will be the main key to success in your field.

The United States of America is, socially and economically, the most powerful country in the world. This economic status was achieved by the actions of a few risk takers. It became the culture of the US to be a risk taker, particularly in the areas of finance, engineering, science, weapons, manufacturing, technical knowledge, medicine, etc. because they believe that there is significant benefit to be gained from taking a risk of the unknown. Although I said earlier it's essential to take a risk based on your experience, don't think I am contradicting myself by now saying something completely different. Let me illustrate this more clearly for you. For example, if someone tells you that they are travelling from London to the US next week, initially you would think they will be flying there. However, there are other methods of transport from London to the US without using the air; such as cruise ships and sea vessels. For you, travelling to the US by air is better but it doesn't mean there is no other option. We like to operate in our comfort zones but sometimes it's better to take other paths so that in life we can make more meaningful progress.

On 15th January 2009, the US Airways flight 1549, an Airbus A320, successfully landed on the Hudson River in New York. The emergency situation of this flight started three minutes after take-off when a flock of birds struck the plane engines during the take-off. Both engines on the aircraft lost power and failed to work. The two experienced pilots had to make an emergency landing on the water, and they and their crew successfully saved the lives of all 155 passengers. Can you imagine the horrible feelings going through the minds of those two pilots, particularly when they realised the power of those two engines would not help them reach the nearest airport? They took a risk and it worked, which made them heroes for life.

In the early 1960s, youths from sub-Saharan Africa would risk their lives and travel to the West African country of Sierra Leone to work in the diamond mines. Despite facing much danger, they risked everything just to be there, and work in an environment where they had to dig in soft soil to reach diamonds many meters below the surface. In underground tunnels with no safety equipment whatsoever, fatal accidents were a common occurrence and many youths would not see their loved ones again.

Businesses from many nations descended on the Sierra Leone diamond fields to get their own share of the action. Demand for youth employment surged in the area dramatically. Thousands of people got rich through that lucrative business; the Sierra Leone diamond boom created opportunity for many local land owners and communities.

The financial benefit to be gained from diamond mining exacerbated the desire among youths to take even more risk to explore the riverbeds to find diamonds and make the money to feed their families. People who didn't take the risk regretted their lack of action at a later stage. Many West African youths ventured to other countries in the diamond business. From Sierra Leone, people took a risk and went to Liberia, Guinea Conakry and the Ivory Coast. In the late 1960s they went even further afield to Europe.

The diamond boom in the West Africa by black Africans was nothing other than people's willingness to take a risk in order to improve their lives. Similar pursuit of wealth is prevalent in history: the 18th century Australian gold rush, the 17th century America sugar and cotton rush and the 15th century Africa and Middle East gold rush, for example.

Risk doesn't always follow your expectations; but someone else will always benefit. For example, a pensioner takes an unknown risk by investing his life savings on the stock market and expecting to gain a big reward. In the end he could lose the whole sum without getting any reward. He was inspired to invest in the stock market, his risk didn't work for him and it was the stock market that benefited. Sometimes it's like that: one risk taker benefits at the expense of another risk taker.

But you hope that he would learn from that failure and maybe prepare better before taking the next calculated risk. Failure is not always due to one's own mistakes or someone else's fault but it may happen because of natural disaster, death, illness, etc. The moral obligation laid on the shoulder of each person is to ensure each time while taking a risk, you do it by your own free will, without being pressured by anyone, without greed or envy.

The willingness to use the power of your imagination is very helpful at any time, especially if it is combined with the willingness of taking a risk. Right now as I am writing this book, using my positive imagination, I can guarantee a significant number of my readers are thinking "Oh my God, life is so exciting, it never occurred to me that by using the power of my imagination I could accomplish anything in my life without fear of failure, and I could magically transform my dreams to amazing reality."

This might trigger the following question from you: why is Yaya taking the risk on his reputation by assuming that he can read people's thoughts in advance? No, I am not risking my reputation; all I am doing is taking a risk based on my experience.

Don't forget I said that I would frequently challenge you. So before we reach the next chapter, I would like to check we all know the meaning of taking an unknown risk, with four examples.

1. If you have $5000, and you want to invest it to generate at least $10,000 in six months, let's say you have four options where you can put your money: livestock, property, transport, or banking. Where will you risk your money? I guess most people will be comfortable to take a risk with banking, property and transport because they are assets, not liabilities; livestock is a liability. However, I would rather take a risk on livestock. The logic behind that is this: the essence of taking a risk is taking an intellectual gamble on something with the expectation that it would deliver an amazing reward. Investing in something which is clearly guaranteed to give you a reward is not a risk at all, it's just investment.

Investing in banking, property and transport is almost guaranteed to deliver a reward because it usually comes with insurance. Investing in them does not involve huge risk, but investing in livestock is highly risky investment because insurance does not usually cover it. However, depending on your culture, I think your chances of generating more income from livestock investment are higher than other three areas I mention above. Also, your chances of losing revenue in livestock investment are higher than the other three areas. When it comes to taking an unknown risk, always have the desire to gamble on something which could give you a higher reward. But it's entirely up to you. You can use the power of your positive imagination to determine which investment you would choose from these four.

2. If fire happened to engulf your home, you didn't have water to put it out and your children were inside, what would you do? Usually in such an emergency, the authorities would recommend you seek the professional help of the police and fire service. However, I would risk everything to rescue my children no matter what, then afterwards I would seek professional help. The rational thinking behind my risk is that I have lived almost half my life already and my children have potential for the future, therefore they have more reasons to survive. They deserve every single drop of my blood. If anything bad happened to them I would blame myself forever.

But it's worth remembering in certain circumstances, human intervention does not save lives. The New York World Trade Center disaster as result of terrorist attack and the fire disaster in London's Grenfell Tower are exceptionally rare occurrences. In these rare circumstances, fire fighters risked everything to rescue people from the inferno but despite their best efforts, it was not enough to prevent the significant loss of life and property. Can you imagine distraught parents throwing their children from the top windows of skyscrapers, genuinely hoping that they will manage to make it to safety? In that atmosphere, the situation is totally beyond imagination as well as human solution; only through the intervention of God could a miracle happen. Sometimes when human beings faces certain circumstances in life, all they can do is hope, pray and give comfort to each other.

The concept of "I am willing to take a risk" in an emergency situation only makes sense in the situations where you truly believe human intervention is going to make a difference and you genuinely feel that your actions would be beneficial. Once again use the power of your positive imagination to draw your own conclusion.

3. Can you imagine losing a wonderful job just because you are late due to heavy traffic on the way to work? A new job with an attractive salary which you recently managed to get for yourself but your boss had abundantly made it clear to you that if you are even five minutes late coming to work, you will get the sack immediately. Living with such a heart-breaking dilemma, one Monday morning you leave the house heading to work. Unfortunately you are one hour behind schedule, and you are stuck in the morning rush hour traffic; however, there are a few chances to jump the queue and drive through a red light. Would you seize that opportunity? For me, I would rather take the risk of losing my job than putting my life and the lives of many other road users at risk. If you take your job seriously enough, every day you should try to leave home as early as possible in order to avoid the morning rush hour. Also, you have a choice to accept the terms and conditions of your work. In my opinion losing your job should not result in losing your life. But taking a risk on your life might cause you to lose your life as well as lose your job. In the end with your imagination, you can be your own judge.

4. Can you imagine waiting many months for a response

from a university you had applied to, with the intention to undertake a four year masters degree course in commerce, but you hear nothing? While you are waiting to hear from the university, amazingly, one of the major high street banks offers you a full time job. Can you imagine being lucky enough to start that job in banking with an amazing opportunity of very good wages at the end of every month? But suddenly the university you had applied to accepts your application; however, while working full time in the bank you are not allow to study full time in the university. What would you do in this fascinating scenario? I think it's better to leave this question unanswered here, so that you can use your imagination to determine whether you would take the risk!

Now, I have shown four different kinds of risk: monetary risk, physical risk, employment risk, and intellectual risk; therefore I am now challenging you to use the power of your positive imagination by contemplating what would you do in these four different situations. Perhaps one day you will come face to face with this kind of situation where you must take a similar risk without having any time to second guess the outcome. Before carrying on reading, pause for a while, and think about what you might do. This is all about enhancing your mental ability to discover your natural talents which will strengthen your confidence and help you appreciate your own intelligence.

The most dangerous risks

A few centuries back, thousands of Europeans risked their lives to explore the world, particularly Africa and America, for greener pastures, in order to alleviate the poverty and social deprivation which engulfed Europe at the time. Later in the 17th century, the same search brought them to Asia and Australia. In the end their gamble paid off; they succeeded in their quest as got the reward.

From the late 1990s to early 2017, thousands of young Africans, mainly from sub-Saharan Africa, risked everything, just like those sixteenth century Europeans, by taking a most dangerous route in small boats across the ocean. The number of African youths risking their lives by taken such dangerous journey dramatically increased from almost 10% per annum to 50%, particularly during 2010 to 2016. The abject poverty, desire of a modern day flamboyant life style, lack of job opportunity and civil war in Libya had exacerbated the figure to jump from mere 10% to almost 50% per annum.

The shocking number of youths undertaking mass migration had escalated to a national emergency for many countries in the continent like Gambia, Ghana, Nigeria, and Eritrea. Young men and women risked crossing the Mediterranean Sea to mainland Italy, Spain, Sicily, Malta and Greece. As a result families were warned by the government not to allow their youths to leave the country.
I know of more than two hundred youths from in and around my own village, Sutukung, who left for Europe. Most of them are now settled in Italy, Germany, France and Greece. From my own perspective I think their willingness to take such a dangerous journey was necessary for human advancement, because while living in Africa a high proportion of these youths were not socially or economically productive, but once in Europe, the majority of them are now learning to become engineers, social workers, architects and small business owners.

I will change the subject slightly by forensically examining risk properly in order to determine what taking a dangerous risk means to you. The literal meaning of taking a risk may vary from culture to culture or have a different context. What is considered financial risk might not be considered material risk.

This is how I would define the meaning of risk: "blindly committing to something with expectation of a positive outcome, yet the outcome is shrouded in uncertainty." Whenever someone is taking an action like this, they know that they are taking a risk. Frequently taking such commitment in all your actions is an important step towards success. Risk takers are the most successful people in the world. You cannot fail to attain success if you are willing to take a risk in all your affairs.

Readers may wonder how often someone has to take a risk. In my opinion, I think that is entirely depending on lifestyle. For instance, professional drivers might take a risk on exceeding the speed limit at every single hour of the day. Yet professions like doctors might take a risk on treating a patient with a transmitted disease once every year. A police officer might take the risk tackling a dangerous criminal every night on duty. A banker might take the risk on gambling public funds every single week. However, compulsive behaviour like taking double risks at the same time would not be considered wise e.g. a driver using mobile phone while exceeding the speed limit, a banker gambling public funds in the casinos as well as the stock market, a married man having an affair with a married woman, a footballer with one yellow card dangerously tackling another player on the football pitch and a parent leaving a child alone in the room with a known paedophile. There are certain risks which I consider very stupid, such as a drug trafficker crossing the border with fake travel documents, a 50 year old having an inappropriate affair with an underage person, a fugitive driving the vehicle without a valid driving licence, a person using a fake document to secure a loan from a bank as well as investing funds with a known criminal.

Some risks are legal and some illegal. Equally, some risks

are ethical, some unethical. Some risks are technical, and some simple. For instance, gambling a large amount of cash in the casino is legal in many countries but avoidance of paying tax on a large amount of cash is illegal. Gambling with cash might bring financial reward and paying tax on that is for your own moral comfort. But you may have the opinion that paying tax on gambling profits is a waste of money. Equally, from the Islamic perspective, the risk of marrying more than one wife is ethical, but risking having an affair with someone is not. From the Christian perspective, risking marrying somebody is ethical, but divorcing them is not. But in the end the fulfilment gained from each risk is that which I call success. Taking massive risks like arms trafficking, human trafficking, drug trafficking, or armed robbery usually results in facing life time consequences. Meaningful reward gained from those high risk areas would only come after successfully laundering the criminal rewards through the banking system in order to legitimise them. You can argue that millions of people are living a comfortable life depending on none other than criminal enterprises. In some cases their living standard is even better than those who gain survival through legitimate means. I can see that this is often the case.

In every risky situation, it's extremely important to use the power of your positive imagination by ensuring that your actions, your choices, and your decisions are always guided by wisdom as well as logic and rational thinking. The right consciousness behind every action will determine the outcome of that particular action, positive or negative. As the saying goes "the same opportunity never appears twice" equally, don't repeat the same failed action. Remember my earlier phrase "making mistake is acceptable but making frequent mistakes is foolishness." Learn from your mistakes.

I love to weigh up the risk before I take it just to make sure I know that I will be able to handle the stress which comes with it. In addition, I will suggest a manageable risk is more desirable than a complex one. Intelligent peoples always measure the weight and the size of the risk they intend to take before taking it. By making a serious commitment, whether it's financial, material or social, always make sure you emotionally measure the scale of the risk to determine whether you will be to handle it or not.

Don't rely on mere good luck and superstition; in the long run such concepts will disappoint you. However, seeking divine intervention through prayers, giving charity and using holy water might help to boost your confidence. No matter how much wealth you possess, or how much luck you have and how highly intelligent you are, always endeavour to seek divine intervention in all your affairs. Remember the most common language use by all politicians in the U.S is "God bless America" - a blessing from God is vital in everything.

Pessimistic behaviour like feeling sad, frequent complaints of bad luck, constant lack of confidence etc does not enhance the power of positive imagination. In some exceptional cases such a negative attitude may as result from illness or a past traumatic event - if you find yourself in that situation, I would recommend you seek professional help. Maybe see a doctor for treatment, have physical therapy from a specialist or seek spiritual counselling. To release the negative energy from your body, I will discuss some emotional techniques in addition to physical exercises which I have often used in the past and recommended to many others. So far these techniques have proved very effective.

Before I share these with you, can you pause and use the power of your positive imagination to answer the following questions. Do animals have a sense of humour? If so, could you provide the list of animals that have the sense of humour? And do animals laugh? Do animals use different languages like human beings? Again like humans beings, do animals learn from each other's language? Why don't scorpions and snakes travel in groups like birds and mammals do? Finally, why do human beings of different skin colour have the same shadows? I am sure you will answer these questions very easily.

Now, let me demonstrate the techniques by first giving you some tips. Please recognise that timing is the key to everything; whether it's about timing for pregnancy, timing for taking a risk, timing for investment .. timing is the key to everything, I cannot emphasise this enough. There is a good time to do things, and a bad time.

Let's talk about good timing. I need your emotional strength and concentration on what am about to share with you, otherwise you will not the benefit from it. You don't have to be from a particular faith to practise it. I invented this ritual for my personal wellbeing, to strengthen my spiritual growth and I have practised it for many years now. I realised this technique is very useful to enhance the power of imagination. I recommended it to some of my clients, and so far I have received some impressive testimonials.

On many different occasions, I wanted to find out what are the causes of depression, which is the enemy of the positive power of imagination. I recognised that the emotional constraints of depression are not always for medical reasons but they are often spiritual matters and they could be treated by using a simple method such as my technique. People have benefitted from it.

Here is the technique, which I call 'Enlighten 9-12-3-6'

This enlightenment technique has three sessions. Each session is for three days, at four distinct times each day. Three sessions of three days makes this a nine day course.

Session One

Part one: choose a day to begin. When you wake up in the morning, follow your normal routine, have breakfast, brush your teeth etc, and then make sure you step out of your home at exactly 9 o'clock in the morning. Go out for walk around public places such as train stations, bus stops, markets, etc for at least half an hour. While walking, make sure you use the power of your positive imagination by visualizing yourself as very successful in whatever field you prefer. 9 a.m. is the time when successful people are out and about pursuing their dreams, and people are going about their daily lives. It has become a tradition for most countries to adopt 9 a.m. as the hour to start work. This hour is associated with a certain energy which enhances imagination. Stepping out of your house at this hour is an opportunity for you to associate yourself with positive and creative thinking people, which means soon you will become one of them.

People use different methods to exercise their mind, body and soul. Some people use jogging to exercise to enhance their physical strength as well as emotional wellbeing. Others may use music, while some others listen to religious texts like the holy Quran or the holy bible during their exercise. I don't use any of the above. Whenever I do my Enlighten 9-12-3-6, I don't use any aids to enhance my imagination. Hearing music or listening to someone reading might distract me from focusing on my goals and it could also affect my concentration when I visualize my success. I shift all my attention to visualisation of my goals and how soon I can achieve them. The best weapon for creative thinking is tuning in to your imagination and listening to your heart while contemplating deeply to reach your inner strength.

Using this exercise, positive feelings will come to your mind and creative thinking will automatically follow.

Part two: at 12 o'clock in the afternoon, find yourself a nice quiet place to meditate for at least half an hour. While meditating, use the power of positive imagination to visualize your success. At midday, positive thinking people are physically and emotionally resting, schoolchildren are having their lunch break, and intelligent people are reflecting on their experience from the morning. At lunch time, too much positive energy is associated with this hour. The usual advice for people doing mediation is this; follow your breathing thoroughly and focus on your intuition at all times. While doing meditation, it's extremely important to contemplate the positive things you gained from your morning exercise, as well as the good memories gained from jogging in the park, say. Hopefully by now, you are much more enlightened than you were yesterday morning.

Part three: at 3 o'clock in the afternoon, have a nap for at least an hour. During the nap, if you have dreams, try to hold them in your memory and when you wake up, make a note of the dreams you had and compare them to your real life goals. In order for you to make sense of your dreams, you might have to ask someone to translate their meaning. This is essential, because most people receive messages from God through their dreams, particularly during their afternoon nap. The subconscious mind passes information to the conscious mind and as a result people get information through their dreams.

Part four: at 6 o'clock in the evening, make sure you step out of your home on the dot. Now you are approaching the final exercise for the day. Repeat exactly what you did in the morning; go out for walk for half an hour, but visit different places to the morning. If you had jogged around the local park, now try jogging around the market. At 6 p.m. millions of successful people are now leaving work and returning home to their families and friends. In the afternoon, they had engaged in business. While you are out there, you can mingle with successful people and engage with the positive energy at their disposal and their mental capacity, which will prepare you to becoming one of them.

You have now completed the first session of Enlighten 9-12-3-6. Now let's quickly summarise it. Choose to start Enlighten 9-12-3-6 on any day of the week. On that day, leave your home at 9 a.m. to exercise for at least 30 minutes, do your meditation at 12 p.m., have your afternoon nap at 3 p.m., and go out for your final exercise at 6.pm. Repeat this for three consecutive days, without missing a single day.

Whenever you are ready to do this method of exercise, do it in a way that works for you. You might wonder how to do this exercise if you are working the afternoon - here is my advice to you. No one is under any obligation to do something which might harm your social or professional life. However, there are maybe times when you would need a break from that life in order to spiritually enhance your emotional as well as physical wellbeing. During this period of soul-searching, you will need a clear conscience with clear vision so that you might bring your life back in order once more.

In order to do that in my opinion, taking nine days leave from work to enhance your spiritual as well as material growth is more than necessary. No matter how wealthy you are, or how intelligent you become, to achieve more, there is always room for improvement. But nothing is written in stone: it's entirely up to you to find your own way.

Session Two

Once again in this session there are four parts but the method is different to session one.

Part one: after finishing all your usual morning tasks, make sure that you are ready to start at 9 a.m. sharp. Sit somewhere quiet and write down the goals you intend to achieve in the coming years, including any ideas generated from session one. While you are writing your list, take your time and use the power of your positive imagination to visualize taking action and pursuing your dreams. Alternatively, you can use a voice recorder on your phone to make your list. When you finish your list, keep it somewhere safe.

Part two: at 12 o'clock in the afternoon, find someone who you really trust, like a spouse, family member, friend, or teacher. Share your ideas with them and ask their genuine opinion on how to achieve your goals. Please note that asking someone to express their opinion on your ideas doesn't mean your life is totally depending on their approval. Seeking advice from loved ones is an effective tool to boost your confidence and check whether your goals are achievable or not. Seek advice from people who are not jealous or envious of you. Sharing your ideas with people you trust is very important. I love the famous quote "no man is an Island" - to achieve your goals you will always need help from other people. Always seek help from others.

Trust me, there are millions of genuine people out there

who will offer their help. If people trust you with their ideas and tell you their lifetime goals, don't rubbish their ideas, be dismissive to them, ridicule them or be judgmental for no obvious reason. As a responsible person, always when people share information with you, don't focus on the headlines, but concentrate on the details to ensure your conscience is clear in providing genuine advice.

Part three: just like session one, at 3 p.m. rest while contemplating your goals and determine where you need to make changes in your life. In case if you don't have a desire to nap in bed that afternoon, try to do something useful like reading a newspaper, magazine or book to generate more ideas, or research online the stories and techniques of successful people. If you find a good story, adopt that person as a role model, and follow their example. This way you will add more purpose to your meaningful life. Sometimes people lack ambition because they have no admiration of a role model.

Part four: at 6 p.m. step out from your home and stroll for a while, then find a nice spot to sit and relax in a public place like a restaurant, cafe, bar, or public park. Brainstorm using the power of your positive imagination by watching people move around you; while you do, concentrate more their behaviour, because every single detail about a person's behaviour should interest you. Dealing with peoples in real life requires knowledge of human behaviour. The very people you are now observing include successful people, wealthy people, poor people, sick people, healthy people, and ordinary people. Which groups of people do you want to belong to?

Many people are doing the same thing as you by striving for success. Success depends on the amount of effort people are prepared to put in to their action plan.

Remember the football match between Manchester City and Liverpool? Each team is a very good team with a successful record, but in the end, Manchester City won because of their extra hard work, team work with team spirit, and determination with dedication to win no matter what.

Now let's quickly summarise session two. At 9 a.m. write down your ideas and the goals you ae pursuing, at 12 p.m. share those ideas with someone you trust, rest or read interesting stories at 3 p.m., and go out to observe people at 6.pm. Repeat session two for three consecutive days, without missing a single day.

Session Three (the final session)

In session one, you exercised your mind, body and soul to generate more ideas and strengthen your emotion and motivation to pursue your goals. In the second session, you set your goals, consulted with people you trust, and observed people.

Now it's time for you to take action on my ideas.

Part one: at 9 a.m. put the ideas you gained from the past six days into action. To do that entirely depends on what you are pursuing right now; for example, if your goal is to get a job, act on it by going online to search for jobs and send emails with your CV to employers. Check newspapers that advertise jobs in your local area. Try to spend a significant amount of time on this until you get a response. Of course your goal might not be to find a job. It could be anything; auctioning a business plan, seeking education, making better use of leisure time, and much more. While you are taking action on anything, it is crucial you imagine yourself as being very successful. Success never happens by accident; influential people, wealthy people, powerful people and inspirational people all imagined themselves being successful long before they attained success.

Part two: at 12 p.m. check your email to ensure you haven't missed anything important. Keep checking.

Part three: at 3 p.m. have a rest for at least two hours. While resting, you can plan your next move from there with a lot of care. Although you might be very eager to attain instant success, but putting your ideas into practise is not about instant success. Neither is it about putting pressure on yourself or feeling jealous and envious of other people. It's all about taking action with effort, which will eventually deliver success for you, with no time limit to that. As usual every long journey starts with the first step which requires massive strength, both emotional and physical.

Part four: at 6 p.m., take the final step to accomplish your goals. At this time in the evening, most people have already returned home from work. It's time for you to step out and engage people in conversation. If it's necessary, at this stage request favours from people who you think have power and influence. Your willingness to interact with influential and powerful people will go a long way towards rewarding you by accomplishing your dreams.

When you achieve your goals through this Enlighten 9-12-3-6 technique, the exercise can remain part of your life forever. By completing this final session for three consecutive days, you have reached the end of Enlighten 9-12-3-6.

Now let's quickly summarise session three. At 9 a.m. take action on your goals and check the progress you made on your actions, at 12 p.m. checking your emails, rest to generate more ideas at 3 p.m., and engage people to boost your chances through networking at 6.pm.

A positive mind is the key to self-esteem

In every culture, people use different techniques to generate more ideas, and have rituals to gain good luck. While I was researching the concept of good luck I saw that, in some societies like Africa, Middle East and Asia it's a habit when looking for opportunities or searching for happiness to look for certain signs before proceeding.

For example some Africans believe that when searching for a job or business, if the first person they meet in the street is female that means they will have good luck. But if the first person they meet is male, then that means bad luck is waiting for them. Some people believe that you should only go out when sun is shining or wind is blowing in a particular direction or they look for a particular bird standing in this or that position. In the past, this kind of concept was prevalent, but in modern Africa it's less significant. In my opinion success is not determined by superstition but by what is contained in your brain. For most intelligent people, success is totally depending on the quality of your choices and how effectively you manage to executed your actions. People send their children to school and university to enhance their imagination so that they can make good choices. Better imagination would surely lead to a better consciousness, and better consciousness will lead to a clear vision which is the key to solving every human need.

Most superstitions are useless and won't generate anything meaningful for you. They only lead to misery, laziness, pessimism and poverty. Taking this road to self-destruction is dangerous for you. The techniques I share with you are not superstition; they are a practical exercise to enhance the power of imagination which is essential for human advancement.

Attaining a life time goal is not linked to who you first meet in the street one morning or which direction the wind blows. It is dependent on the choices you make and the timing in which you put those choices into practise. Good planning in advance will also reward you. It is okay to keep changing your plans until you make the right choice, but to keep changing your goals is not wise.

For example, one of the goals I set in 2017 was to complete three books; but my plans about which subjects to write about changed. You might set a goal to enrol in university to study medicine, but your plan to study medicine might change to study law instead. Changing your plan does not affect your goal to enrol at university this year; do you see what I mean?

People's plans can change but their goals should not change. Self-esteem is really crucial in your decision making process, particularly when it comes to planning. People with a high degree of self-esteem are more confident in their actions than those who have a negative view of themselves. For instance, people with revolutionary minds stand more chance of earning a leadership position in society than people with stagnated minds. Everybody has imagination, but having imagination alone is not enough to become productive: imagination should be combined with positive thinking.
Working to improve yourself mentally and emotionally would create many opportunities for you without constantly depending on people for guidance. Equally, no matter how effective your guidance is, without strong mental and emotional ability to back it up, you cannot sustain the value of that guidance.

Luck is the fruit of a miracle, it doesn't always happen

when expected, yet some peoples are luckier than others. My take on this is that some people are more effective in setting and executing their plans. The more effective the plan, the luckier you will be. For example, it is a widely held belief in many societies that, during the period of a full moon, people claim to feel luckier than usual; also more crime is committed during that period than normal. This concept is widespread even in the contemporary Western society, in addition to ancient Europe. I believe Mother Nature has ability to influence human behaviour, good or bad.

From my own observation I recognised that due to negative pressure from cool weather, people living in a cool environment like Europe and America are more aggressive and crueller than people living in Africa and the Middle East. On the other hand, due to negative pressure from hot weather, people living in a hot environment like Africa and the Middle East are harsher and angrier than people living in Europe and America. In the positive aspect, people living in the cool environment are more patient and focused than people living in a hot environment. People living in the hot environment are more kind and humble than people living in a cool environment. Let's examine this theory in a broader context.

Here is my point: in order to handle negative energy from the cool weather, people living in a cool environment are more likely to be involved in substance abuse like excessive alcohol use, drugs abuse, heavy smoking, etc to keep them warm and calm. Thus the result of using these substances is that violent behaviour is always part of the norm. Aggressive attitudes such as domestic and child abuse and animal cruelty are frequently a common occurrence in those societies. Such behaviour will usually end with harsh punishment which I call "bad luck". By contrast, the positive energy from the cool weather often causes people to think better and focus on what they are doing as well as being more patient to make more progress. Consequently people living in that cool environment are smarter, more intelligent, and confident than people living in the hot environment. That is what I called "good luck".

On the other side of my argument: the negative energy from the hot weather usually gives people high blood pressure which is the recipe for constant anger and irrational behaviour. Thus those living in a hot environment are angrier and harsher, which exposes them to civil disobedience, family conflicts, resentment towards one another, and other unacceptable erratic behaviour. In order to control such irrational behaviour, some people use substances like alcohol, drugs, tobacco, etc. Using them in that hot environment only adds more fuel to the fire and as a result disaster is a common occurrence. That is what I call "bad luck". By contrast, the positive energy from hot weather would cause people living in that environment to be more kind and humble. People living in a hot environment are more likely to share their wealth with others, as well as being physically more attractive and humble than people living in a cool environment. That is what I call "good luck". Energy generated from Mother Nature either is good or bad energy, and it can greatly influence people's actions and their behaviour, which may cause good luck or bad luck for them.

I remember when I was a child, in the night time during the full moon we used to stay awake longer than usual, particularly during the spring and autumn season. In the middle of the night when the moon was shining, we used to play certain games which make us happier than games we played during the period of dark nights. For villagers like me, moonlight is a privilege because there are no other sources of light at night other than the moonlight; moonlight is associated with good luck. Sea water is good luck for those living in land-locked countries but is normal for people living in coastal areas. People like me born in a hot country would find it challenging to handle cool weather, and as result they would associate cool weather with bad luck.

Peoples living in black society often associate black and red with bad luck, and white and green with good luck. By contrast, white people would usually associate blue and white with good luck, rather than black and brown. Consequently weddings with white and blue dress are more preferable to many than any other colour, while at funerals, black and brown are more preferable than any other colour.

In places like Africa and the Caribbean, people with white skin or fair complexion particularly in women are more preferable than those with dark skin. White skin is privilege in a black society. Hence in black weddings, wearing a white colour is more attractive than wearing the any other colour. Different cultures have a different view. Wearing white at a funeral has more of a religious aspect.. that is, depending on which religion you follow. Perhaps culture and religion dictate people's behaviour more than anything else. Good and bad luck depends on belief systems. What is perceived to be good luck in one culture is not necessary perceived to be good luck in any other culture. What causes bad luck in one culture might not cause bad luck in others.

But what remains the same in every culture and always makes a great impact is individual self-esteem, which enhances people's confidence to trust themselves, the physical and emotional ability to take action on their ideas, good planning before executing those ideas, and the individual choices people make before taking action. This would definitely make a difference in bringing good or bad luck to both you and society.

There are number of places associated with the concept of good energy and bad energy. This might sound like superstition to you, but in reality it is entirely different.

To me, superstition is when you associate times, colours, places, patterns or objects with good or bad luck without the support of physical or spiritual energy. But times, colours, places and objects can have energy. My Enlighten 9-12-3-6 exercises have energy in them, hence they are universally accepted by my clients to be an effective source of good energy, and therefore they are associated with good luck. Blue skies, flowers, natural water, gold and silver rings, rainwater in the summer, gemstones and diamonds, colours of objects and spiritual amulets all have good energy. Using these things for good purposes is common in every society because they hold good energy and they may also serve to boost the power of your imagination. However, they work in different ways for different people.

Let's examine how one of these things works for people with the power of imagination. When people are going out during the day while the sky is clear and blue, the positive energy coming through the sunlight helps the human body to store vitamin D, which is an essential contribution to human advancement, especially to emotional strength and helping the body to relax. The positive feeling from sunlight pushes your confidence through the roof, which I consider as good luck for you.

Positive energy which is produced by each of the above will effectively improve your physical and emotional wellbeing. Additionally, it boosts the power of your intuition to see the chaotic world around you differently.

I remember from my childhood, one positive aspect of using my imagination was the association of unseen patterns and objects with a particular colour. I associated each day of the week with a particular colour, places I had never seen to a particular familiar place I had known, and names of people I had never seen to particular attributes I could imagine.

My favourite colours are black, brown, white, yellow and green. My least favourite colours are red, purple, grey, and pink. I think my favourite colours are lucky, and the others are not. This maybe sounds a bit strange to you, but it worked for me. Whenever I heard the word Monday, I associated that day with white, when I heard Tuesday, I associated that day with brown. Wednesday was black, Thursday pink, Friday yellow, Saturday bright white and Sunday dark brown. Whenever I took action on a particular day I associated my action with each colour, and good or bad luck. I am sure I am not alone in associating colours with days. But, despite this, I made sure it didn't interfere with my everyday life by carrying on with my affairs, even if the day was thought to hold bad luck.

When people mention names that are not familiar to me, or I hear names of places where I have never been before, in order to make sense of that, usually I would associate the people with somebody I already know or the place to somewhere I am familiar with. For example when I was a young man if someone mentioned "Hong Kong" it reminded me of the bush farms where we used to cultivated ground nuts, thus I used my imagination to associate Hong Kong with that particular farm. Hence, for me, the country called Hong Kong is always associated with positive energy. By contrast, whenever I hear the name "Silicon Valley", I associate that place with bad weather, particularly when it's raining, with thunder and lightning. I've never visited either place, but I have already painted a picture of them which is associated with positive and negative energy as well as good or bad luck.

Although there is no factual evidence available to me to support these theories, yet by spiritually associating things with objects, materials and colours familiar to me, I hope to give purpose and comfort to my readers, many of whom are pursuing good ways to better use their imagination. And until we reach our goal, nothing should prevent us from pursuing that energy with which we will attain success.

The third reason why you cannot fail to succeed

Be willing to take action on your ideas. As I said before, people who have passion about their ideas will take action on them to show the world they are capable, talented and competent.

You may be attracted to a beautiful girl living in your neighbourhood who you would like to date, yet approaching her is difficult for you. The guy next door may be more willing to take action, so he stands more chance of winning her heart.

If someone is praying to have a child with his newly wedded bride, if he has no desire in being physically intimate with her, surely she will never get pregnant by him. Wishful thinking doesn't always work for everyone but taking action works for everyone.

Most people don't get their dream job because they feel lazy and don't take action. When you travel to countries with emerging economies like India and Brazil, you will come to realise their society is more willing to act on ideas.

Societies with willingness are much happier, smarter, and more confident.

You might wonder why some people are luckier and more advanced than others, and why some societies are wealthier and more advanced than others. Here is my opinion, although I am not a natural scientist in any discipline, but I am a keen observer of Mother Nature and my own surrounding. Just by observing the environment, I realised weather patterns are different everywhere around the world. Some countries are cooler than others, and some are more environmentally friendly than others. For now just forget about what you have learnt from science.
Every country receives sunlight from the sky, moonlight from the sky, rain from the sky and wind from the atmosphere. These natural gifts from God are all coming from the same solar system, but why do some communities receive more benefit from them than others? And why are they more destructive for some communities (typhoons and hurricanes, say) and less destructive for others (dehydration caused by high temperature and skin problems caused by sunlight)?

Energy from weather patterns in the atmosphere influences human behaviour and also mental and physical wellbeing. This is not just my own theory but has been scientifically proved. According to some scientists, during the full moon the tide rises to a higher level than usual. Certain patterns in the weather on particular times of day, week, month and year could be crucial to the outcome of your success because maybe your natural alertness is more effective at certain times. In the United Kingdom people are advised not to drive between the hours of 11 p.m. to 6 a.m. because at this time, natural alertness may be lower than usual.

This piece of advice proved my theory that there are good

and bad times for doing things. For example, people searching for a job at the beginning of the month, let's say from the 1st to the 15th, are more likely to find a job quickly than those who search from the 15th to the 30th. Additionally, people who look for a job at the beginning of the week from Monday to Thursday are considered more serious than those who try to look from Friday to Sunday. Basically if two people had the same opportunity, the person who acts with careful planning will have double the chance to excel than a person who doesn't.

The example from Mother Nature is enough to inspire people to act in a timely way on their ideas.

However, on the other hand some may equally argue; why do some soils have more natural fertility while other soils needs fertiliser in order for them to produce better crops, while they all use the same rain water? Why are certain seasons more effective to cultivate seed and harvest food? The argument continues: why is one child more successful that another, if they are born into the same family? Why are people born in some countries more successful than others? Why are people born at a certain time of year more also successful than others?

The logic response to this argument is that; human beings are unique and some people are more successful than others because some people are born more talented than others. Conspiracy theorists would tell you they are luckier, and that is why they are more talented and they will be more effective in taking action to pursue their goals. Hence with this argument, you cannot rule out the power of luck. What about those who don't have good luck? I think they must take action to use the power of positive imagination to find other alternatives in order for them to succeed.

Religious opinion might differ from the above. It may say that God created everything, good and bad, and all human success only comes through the will of God, it has nothing to do with individual talents and effort. The superstitious would say success is due to luck. The logical would say it is all due to talent and effort. None of these opinions solve the essence of this argument, because each camp fails to provide facts to back their claim.

In my opinion, from a religious perspective, while is possible for people to use fertiliser in dry lands to nourish the soil, then it is entirely possible for people to use holy substances including the power of prayer as a blessing to nourish their luck and become more fortunate in attaining good luck. Equally, superstitious people could use energy sources, including amulets, to enhance their luck in order for them to achieve whatever they want in life. And people in the logic camp may continue to pursue their luck through using talent and effort. However, no matter which camp you belong to, your desire to conquer luck would require you to take action.

In relation to this topic of talent and luck, I conducted research to check the background of the most powerful people in the world, to determine whether people's pattern of has any significance to their luck and success. This research included political leaders, business people, sports stars, film actors, religious leaders and other wealthy people. I looked at the day they were born, the month and the year. My research was focused on the 52 most influential individuals from different backgrounds living around the world from current and the past generations.

In this research I found that 28 out of 52 were born from 1st to 15th of the month while 24 were born from 15th to 31st of the month. Additionally, 31 among them were born between January and June and the rest (21) born between June and December.

38 of these people had a small number (from 1 to 6) at the end of the year of their birth. For example 1971, the last digit is small (1). Only 14 had a large digit from 7-0 at the end of the year of their birth.

Finally, what I find intriguing was this: if you combine all births from this group, 41 of them all occurred in six particular months. January (9), March (6), May (6), June (6), October (9), and November (5). So January and October had the most births. Just 11 births occurred in four months: February (2), April (2), July (4), and August (3), while none were born in September and December. Out of these 52 peoples, 4 were born on the 1st, 3 on the 9th, 4 on the 14th, 4 on the 17th, 4 on the 19th and 4 on the 26th while other births occurred in a different days. The days where there were no births are the 8th, 10th, 16th, 18th, 20th, 25th and 27th.

When you compared the success rate base on this research, between these two groups it had clearly indicated a significant advantage to those born from the 1st to 15th over those born from the 16th to 31st.

According to the World Health Organisation's report on malaria, which was carried out in Asia and Africa, they found out that people born in certain seasons of the year are more likely to contract malaria than those born in other seasons of the year. In summertime in Africa, malaria is very common in most countries in the continent; people born during this period are more vulnerable to catch malaria than those born in the spring and winter, and there are more mosquitoes. This study by the WHO vindicates my theory and strengthens my position to believe that different seasons have different energies, positive energy for some people and negative energy for others. Being born in a certain season of the year is better than being born in another season.

To illustrate my point further, I would draw your attention to the following sequence of international presidential elections.

George Bush vs Al Gore: George Bush was born 6th July 1946 and Al Gore born 31st March 1948 Bush with a lower date of birth won the 2000 presidential election. Barack Obama vs John McCain: Obama was born 4th August 1961 and McCain born 29th August 1936. Obama with a lower date of birth won the 2008 election. Obama vs Mitt Romney: Romney was born 12th March 1947, again Obama with the lower date of birth won the 2012 election. Very recently Donald Trump vs Hillary Clinton: Trump was born 14th June 1947 and Hillary born 26th October 1947. Trump with a lower date of birth won the 2016 presidential election. Finally, Yahya Jammeh vs Adama Barrow; Jammeh was born 25th May 1965 and Barrow bon 15th February 1965. Barrow with a lower date of birth won the 2016 Gambia presidential election.

Although the high proportion with lower date of birth shown on the example won most elections, equally you can argue then why Marine Le Pen with lower date of birth 5th August 1968, lost the 2017 French election to Emmanuel Macron with a higher date of birth, 21st December 1977. For now you can stick with my theory until you conduct your own research to prove otherwise.

If you boil down my theory it will come down to one main point which is this; taking an earlier action is more advantageous than waiting. My research shows that people born in the month of January and October are luckier than most people. Additionally, people born from the 1st to 15th of the month are the most energetic people. Therefore, if you adhere to such a concept try to get pregnant during the month of May which may guarantee a February date of birth for your child. Getting pregnant in

February may guarantee a November date of birth for your child. However, it is entirely up to you, you can do your own home work by using the power of your positive imagination to determine which date suits you the most.

Your willingness to take action with positive energy, which is usually the source of good luck, is matter of faith, as well as talent and effort.

If a man who never gambled before suddenly decided to play the lottery and he subsequently won the jackpot, why did he win: is it the will of God, good luck, or effort? If his winning is due to the will of God, God doesn't like gambling so why would he arrange for this man to win? If his winning is due to his effort, well, this guy never made an effort to gamble before. On this occasion, I would consider his winning was pure good luck from the action he took.

Consider healthy twin brothers from the same parents, living in similar circumstances with a similar life pattern and healthy life style. However, let's say just after their 50th birthday, one twin dies from a heart attack but the other survived for another 50 years - in this case, what would we consider as the cause to the first twin's sudden death? Would we consider this the will of God or good luck? Perhaps I would consider the survival of the second twin the will of God - mere good luck doesn't cause people to live longer than usual, but the will of God does.
Consider two brothers who graduated from the same university with a degree in business management, however, one brother is more intelligent than other. What would we consider the secret behind his intelligence? I would consider it due to talent and extra effort, because being born to the same parent doesn't guarantee an equal success in everything. Success after graduating from university would usually depend on talent and extra effort.

President Obama's philosophy of success is this:

Move the ball forward, always have hope but don't get complacent and stay focused. Seek help when you can because you can't do it alone. If you are going to commit, commit to something bigger and stop making excuses, but it is essential not to take yourself too seriously. However, stick with your plans and follow your passion.

The fourth reason why you cannot fail to succeed

Learn from your past mistakes. There is a common phrase "He who never makes mistakes never tries anything". I am adding my own phrase to this: "She who often fails without it being her fault will eventually succeed with resilience."

Failure from mistakes is part of everyday life. There is no human society where there is no failure and there is nobody out there who never failed. However, there are millions of people out there who learnt from their failures, and also millions of people who fail to learn from their mistakes.

I said before that making mistakes is considered normal but making frequent mistakes would be considered foolishness. Now your choice is clear: either learn from your mistakes or don't. I would like to discuss this in a broader context; to begin, let's ask ourselves this crucial question: how frequently should I allow myself to fail? How often do people notice my failure? And how often do I fail?

Every aspect of human life is a journey, and every journey comes with its challenges; hence, there will be ups and downs in all journeys. Therefore, whatever you are pursuing, do it with dedication and determination, and trust yourself. At any stage in that journey don't expect failure, but challenges which might be crucial to success, and you won't fail if you take those challenges in good faith. This will help you to prepare yourself emotionally and enhance your psychological ability in order for you to continue with the next stage of the journey with confidence.

While learning from failure, always try to be positive by anticipating a good outcome from all your actions and be ready to face challenges further down the road.

Let me share my own experience with you. People close to me are very familiar with this story so I will share it with you. I cannot remember the exact date, but it was one day in September 1993 when I was around 18 years old, my uncle's friend living in New York City had sent me an invitation to visit his company to receive a special training on how to handle a milling machine. A few days later I went to the U.S. embassy to apply for a non-immigrant visa. Arriving at the embassy at around 7 a.m., I saw approximately three hundred people lining up in long queues waiting to submit their visa application forms. I picked up a form and I gave it to a young lady to complete for me, because in those days I could neither speak or write or read English. She completed my form and handed it to me; then I went back to the queue to continue the application process.

First I had to wait in the queue until I could reach the visa desk to submit my form. Then I had to wait again for an interview. And when it was my turn I submitted my visa application form with all my supporting documents and two small pictures of me. Then I was asked to wait again until my name was called for the interview; can you imagine at this point I was extremely nervous? Trust me, in those days getting a U.S. visa was too much intimidating because the refusal rate was skyrocketing. Nearly 80% of all applicants were refused, particularly young illiterate boys like me. At about 2:30 p.m. they called my name. Immediately I went to the window to face the entry clearance officer. I could see everything behind him, including other people's visa application files, computers, photocopy machines, and two other staff sitting behind the desk helping him process the visa application forms.

I can still vividly remembered how he looked; an average, smart-looking, skinny, tall white man, casually dressed in a white shirt and blue trousers wearing reading glasses, with an unsmiling pointed face. He looked at me and glanced at my documents just for few seconds, and then started to conduct the interview by first asking "What is your name?" in a deep intimidating voice. I nervously replied "I can't speak English, sir." "You cannot speak English?" he reaffirmed, and I said yes. Then he called one of his assistants to come and translate for me.

In a few sentences, said in less than 30 seconds, he asked the assistant to tell me the following - "I am not going to grant you a visa to travel to the U.S.A. because you cannot speak English. How can you communicate with the people there?" Then he opened my passport and stamped the last page with a red stamp which was a common practice at that time. He emphasised that I was not allowed to appeal his decision and I should not attempt any further visa applications for six months. Then he returned my passport and all my documents, except the photos and the application form, and he gave me a visa refusal letter.

At that stage emotionally I was struggling to cope with the anger from such disappointment. Keeping my feet firmly on the ground was almost impossible for me; it felt like I was hit by a heavy truck and suddenly I couldn't feel my body weight anymore. While returning home, I was seriously struggling to keep my balance, and with shock I nearly fainted on the road. When I reached the main gate of the embassy compound I noticed people were staring at me. While heading home I was totally subdued, like a defeated man. When people leave the embassy premises, you can see the difference in their body language: it is not difficult at all to distinguish those who get a visa from those who fail to get one. Can you use the power of your imagination to visualise how I was feeling at that moment? My excitement about going to the U.S. vanished in 30 seconds. My dream of a new life in the U.S. crashed before I had crossed Atlantic Ocean. My disappointment was unbearable. Now, I had to explain what had happened to my family. There were going to be many questions as to why I was refused a visa. The weight of shame for me was so huge. I was wondering in my mind how could that man hurt my innocent soul like this, and I was wishing every bad luck available here on earth on him. From the embassy building I walked 4km all the way to our compound. When I got home, I quickly rushed into my room and took off my dress black business suit and necktie, as sombre as a politician who lost the election.

I learnt later from embassy sources that the entry clearance officer who had rejected my visa application was known to be very strict with the first time visa applicants, particularly young people like me who had no genuine reason to travel to U.S.A. For the benefit of those who have never been through such a visa process in Africa, the heartbreak feeling from visa refusal is equivalent to when a student living in the West fails his or her G.C.S.E examination, or the rejection of a talented singer by the judges presiding over a TV talent show. Can you imagine the huge disappointment people felt at those moments?

From that moment in 1993, it took another seven years for me to get a visa to travel to the United Kingdom in August 2000; however that is its own story for another book. I learnt a lot from this particular failure, including the importance of being able to speak English, and preparing myself in advance by building my confidence. Rather than keep blaming the entry clearance officer for my failure, immediately I promised myself this: I will make sure I never get rejected in future just because I can't speak English. From that day on I made sure I worked hard on my English. You can learn from this experience: failure is part of human life, you will fail occasionally, maybe even frequently, but rather than blame others for your failure, try to learn from it as much as possible.

Here's another hypothetical situation: say that you went to dinner with your high school sweetheart whom you intended to marry after leaving school. After dinner, when it was time to pay the bill, you asked her to pay it for you. Because of your failure to take responsibility at that crucial time, she realised that you are not good for her. The next day she stopped responding to your text messages. You decided to call her but she is not answering your calls, and she breaks up with you. What would you do the next time you take a girl to dinner? If you are smart, you'd pay the bill. If you don't, you learned nothing from your past experience and this new girl would dump you too.

Perhaps you can argue sometimes people's failures are not always their fault, but the action of other people who are jealous, envious and judgmental and bear a grudge. However, you cannot control other people's attitudes and their negative behaviour, but you can protect your interests by disassociating yourself from them. It's essential to completely withdraw yourself from those who cause you harm, pain, and grievance.

I used to have a client living in Nottingham, UK. No matter what he did or how he did it, failure is was always the end result for him. Consequently he thought someone may have performed black magic on him to destroy his good luck, a concept common in African and Asian communities. By carefully listening to him and analysing his situation properly, I decided to look deeper in to his family background. Through my frequent interaction with him, I recognised that his failure was mostly due to the bullying and judgmental people who surrounded him. I recommended that he totally disassociate himself from those people. He did, and for the first time in three years, the following month he managed to get a full time job. He learnt a valuable lesson to always avoid people who cause him failure.

I knew someone who learnt a valuable lesson which nearly cast a dark shadow on her entire career. In 2012, the lady in question was facing severe financial difficulties in coping with her mortgage. She approached the bank for a loan of approximately £20,000. As usual, the bank asked her to bring six months' pay slips as well as six months' bank statements. Because at that time she didn't have a full time job, she unfortunately decided to provide fake bank statements and pay slips. The bank of course realised that all her supporting documents were fake, and not only refused to grant her the loan but in fact they closed her bank account and informed other banks in the UK not to allow her to open an account for at least six years.

She was devastated with agony and totally distraught. However, when she approached me for advice I told her that as long as the police fraud unit is not involved in her case, it was highly unlikely the bank would take any further measures against her, because such practice is a common occurrence in the banking industry. I asked her to immediately try and open a new bank account in a different bank, additionally, I asked her to make sure she didn't use fake documents in future. By learning this valuable lesson she is doing very well now; her failure at the bank or elsewhere will never be repeated by her.

"I am willing to learn from my failure" is the most resilient statement in the human vocabulary. Most successful business entrepreneurs around the globe, scientists in any discipline, computer engineers, doctors etc. have all once, or more than once, learned from their failure. But constant failure and making mistakes often probably depends on the quality of your experience and which profession you choose for yourself, as well as your mental and emotional ability for problem solving.

Certain professions like banking (involving a gamble on the stock market) or the transportation business (which might involve motor vehicle accidents) carry more risk of failure than other professions.

Additionally if you have never driven a vehicle before, and suddenly you want become a taxi driver, in this the failure is greater than triumph. Failure is inevitable in almost everything, particularly if you fail to learn from those who have already tried and failed. For example, if you have to face a judge in the courtroom, but you are not familiar with the law, even though you consider yourself intelligent enough to represent yourself in court, trust me, you are likely going to fail. Learn from others before taking such a monumental risk. Don't wait to fail if before you fail there is chance to learn from someone beforehand. Intelligent people always have a desire to keep on learning from other people's mistakes, thus they triumph. If you lack experience in the area you intend to excel, please don't be shy to learn from somebody who had more experience than you, so that one day you can become a master.

No matter how many self-help books you might read or how many conferences you attend, failure to focus and improve yourself physically and emotionally will result in failure for you at every turn. I said before that the reasons why most people never succeed include complacency, taking things for granted and low self-esteem. People with these attributes don't learn from other people.

For instance, nowadays due to terror attacks, a lot of people don't like large crowds or flying in an aeroplane. But fear of these two situations doesn't protect anyone from danger, but using your experience to figure out what to do when danger arises makes a significant difference to your personal wellbeing. If you are an experienced flyer, probably you won't be as worried as travellers who have less experience as you. Knowing what to do in advance is much better than dangling in ignorance. When people board an aircraft, the flight attendants would demonstrate safety features before take-off to ensure the every single person on the plane understands what to do in case of an emergency. However, such demonstrations don't prevent any loss of life whenever crashes occur; but knowing what to do in advance gives comfort to many people on the flight.

Sometimes people lose direction and have no stamina when rebuilding their lives after failure. In such a situation it's good to involve yourself in rituals such as fasting, prayers and giving to charity. Human beings cannot survive without spiritual interaction with God, because human failure is not always due to human error but is occasionally the will of God. Thus whenever you encounter trouble in your life journey as well as facing unimaginable difficulties along the way, it is extremely important to humble yourself before God and ask him to unleash all his blessing on you and bestow his protection on your family. Acts of worship when you feel desperate are the most powerful weapon against all types of human misery. No matter how much experience you have or how much intelligence you possess, a natural disaster could occur at any time. Additionally, it is essential to avoid causing harm, humiliation, emotional torture and grievance to innocent people because harming innocent people in any shape or form will eventually catch up with you one way or the other. Perhaps it might come in the form of bad luck here on earth or grievance in the afterlife.

Imagine if you were a student trying to complete your final year at the high school, but you failed to pass all the subjects you had studied - what would be the next step for you? I would suggest the following: repeat the study for at least another year. Contemplate why you failed the exams and what you could have done better. By soul-searching , you will find out your lack of performance is due to lack of serious study and inadequate homework. So read many books as much as possible, research as much as possible and write as frequently as possible. Just following these tips alone might not be enough to pass the exam without focusing on what you learnt in the classroom and paying attention to every single subject. A student who understands the subjects is more likely to pass exams than those who don't. Students who focus on study and concentrate on the teacher are more effective than distracted students. Yet with all this effort, failure might still occur every now and again but whenever it occurs, embrace it with good faith and accept that it is the will of God.

However, if you keep on having luck in your endeavours, do not big up yourself for one second - stay humble and say all praise is due to God. No matter what level you reach, don't look down on people who are less fortunate than you - this is the perfect character of good people.

Learning from other people's failure will significantly reduce the chance of your own failure. In the modern world, learning from other people includes reading the autobiographies of famous people, particularly the areas where they had disclosed their personal experience. You can get access to this information in the local libraries as well as checking online. There is much learning material stored on YouTube, Wikipedia, WikiHow, Facebook and more; these media platforms are the modern day tools which many people use as teaching methods.

For an example if you already possess a revolutionary mind, but your ideas don't materialise, don't hesitate to familiarise yourself with the stories of people like Nelson Mandela, Fidel Castro, Che Guevara and likeminded people. Don't underestimate your abilities; perhaps in the near future people will learn from your legacy as you are learning from the legacy of these legendary figures. But if you fail in your endeavours, equally you will be on record among the people who fail, and in the future children will learn from your failure and talk about it.

If you don't have the strength to do it all by yourself always seek help from within the families and friends. Please remember that is never too late to seek help and support from other people; there is no super human out there who does everything by themselves without human intervention. In reality, every day and night human beings receive help and support from one another. By working together as one powerful force we can triumph together and supporting each other on our weaknesses will equally help us to avoid constant failure. Our unity is our strength and our division is our failure.

Strengthism

While we are learning how to deal with failure, I would like to shift my attention to discuss a theory I developed called "strengthism" which is relevant to this conversation (please note that, you won't find the meaning of strengthism in a dictionary, I have invented this word to support my own social study theory). I first adopted the theory of strengthism back in 2014 when I was doing research on sociology, particularly in the area of marriage and friendship. I realised from my research that every human institution should operate like a company, whether it is companionship like marriage or a monetary institution like a business, strengthism is crucial to success. I used the terminology of strengthism because the strength of each contribution is helping the institution to flourish.

This is how it works. Let's start with the first model: when you establish a company you will always need at least four main pillars; company director, secretary, accountant, and labourer. In order to run the company smoothly, each of these four people need to perform well in order to avoid failure. My director has the strength to run the company, my accountant has the strength to handle the finances, my secretary has the strength to deal with communication, and my labourer has the strength for handling manual work, and finally the owner who has the strength to run the company affairs.

Ideally, rather than using the traditional titles such as secretary and so forth, you can simply refer to each title as a strength. For example you can refer to the secretary as my strength on communication and the accountant as my strength for handling finances etc. From a psychological perspective based on my experience, whenever you refer to someone as 'my strength', automatically that compliment boosts their self-worth, confidence and self-esteem, and would enable each employee to play their role more perfectly than before. People who consider themselves as inferior struggle to perform well, but whenever you acknowledge their talent and strengths, that will enhance their emotional and physical strength to deliver very much. From the method of strengthism, you can see people using their intuition - rather than depending on each other for survival, they are counting on each other's strength to excel in their endeavours.

Strengthism can be used to sustain stability in relationships and marriage

In the modern society, marriage, family affairs, relationships between individuals, casual friendship and community cohesion is mainly dysfunctional, due to lack of strengthism to boost individual self-esteem. Often people in these kinds of relationships perceive each other as a liability rather than an asset. As a result, I recognise that modern men and women don't usually understand each other because they are judgmental on each other before they truly attain the knowledge of each other.

By introducing profound strengthism in every aspect of human society we will drastically reduce the shortcomings and challenges facing these traditional institutions. Let's discuss how to introduce strengthism in marriage.

In order to reduce the divorce rate in our communities, and improve relationships in dysfunctional families, it is essential to introduce strengthism to the early stage of marriage and children's upbringing. Using the traditional methods of culture and religion to inspire married couples to stay together is no longer effective because the values of culture and religion are increasingly less important. Most people are looking for other alternatives to foster peace and tranquillity in their relationships. Because in the 21st century married life is no longer confined to companionship and cohabiting to produce offspring and satisfy each other's sexual desires, it includes partnership, an equal contribution to society and much more.

Let me demonstrate the same technique which I used in

the company model: firstly, each marriage consists of two individuals, wife and husband. Hence let me use the strengthism model by assuming that marriage is like a company. Now I will appoint the husband as the managing director for the marriage and he is in charged with running the marriage. The wife is an accountant: she is in charge of running the financial affairs. Collectively wife and husband can appoint someone who will assume the secretarial position for the marriage – any time when crisis arises in the marriage, he or she will be in charge to mediate and maintain peace and tranquillity. Finally, if there are children in the marriage, they must assume the rule of employees to ensure mum and dad are well looked after. However, each person working in this institution of marriage must endeavour to effectively play the role assigned to them very well. Additionally, using strengthism, it must be clear to everyone in the team that in order to run this institution properly each person is counting on the strength of the others. That is really crucial to success and everyone in this institution should recognise that they are assets, not liabilities.

The main diseases plaguing social institutions such as marriage are individualism and a culture of dependency. It is exactly why I use the theory of strengthism to discourage that. I know in ancient society it was completely normal for one set of people to entirely depend on others for everything: women especially were totally dependent on their husband's income to support the family. However, I recognise that in modern society it is not desirable for most couples to entirely depend on one person for almost everything. Now couples can use the method of strengthism which means working together as a team rather than each individual pursuing their own interest, which would lead to lack of trust and lack of mutual understanding. By constantly depending on one another without acknowledgment of each individual strengths and contribution, there is then the chance for domestic violence, physical abuse or financial exploitation. The cause of most conflict in social institutions such as marriage and family affairs is the issue of finances and material matters. Now you can use the power of your imagination to introduce strengthism to all your social institutions in order to avoid failure.

We always advocate that equal opportunity is guaranteed for everyone but despite that, in my view equality sometimes depends on the ability of each individual person using the strength they possess in order to perform effectively and give that strength to the team.

It is true that, from a religious and cultural perspective, men are always perceived to be the leaders of society and the head of the family. However, in my view this should entirely depend on the person's individual talents and strength to effectively execute that role properly. Therefore I will recommend that whenever families and couples intend to apply strengthism in all their affairs, it's entirely up to them to choose who they can trust the most and assign that person to a particular position, and to ensure it is clear to everyone in the team what is expected from them.

Although there are no easy solutions to the modern day challenges to marriage and families, each society needs to morally support each other emotionally and intellectually to make sure the road map to a peaceful conflict resolution is possible. I believe there are always enough intelligent people around, who are mature enough to find the solution locally, which will enable them to robustly tackle those issues effectively. We can always strive individually to reach a peaceful resolution to ensure our challenges are contained, rather than wait for outside intervention. The culture of dependency on foreign resources in Africa and

Asia significantly damaged indigenous ability to seriously tackle the issues confronting them, such as poverty, internal conflict and ignorance, which is the leading cause of disease, economic problems and family breakdown. In each of these challenges facing society, we can use strengthism in all our endeavours to ensure all stakeholders are equally contributing their strength by looking after each other's interests.

Now I am going to demonstrate how people might introduce strengthism in their marriages. Assume that you had just recently got married to your dream spouse with the intention to stay together forever. Together with your spouse, you find a nice quiet place to make the blueprint for the future of your marriage. At this stage, appoint one person to fill each important position in the marriage - director and accountant, like how a company operates. Suppose you both agreed that the husband is going to assume the position of director. It is entirely up to you guys as to what his responsibilities will be; they could include dealing with matters related to the extended family, paying household bills, the children's welfare, their school fees and much more. If the wife assumes the position of director, again it is entirely up to you to decide her responsibilities.

However, it must be clear to each individual exactly what needs to be done in that position. Once that is decided, together you should approach someone like a community leader, a religious leader or other prominent member in the society and appoint that person to the position of secretary, who will assume the role of mediator. No matter what it is essential to make sure both of you trust this individual, because from now on that person is going to be your guiding angel whenever trouble and misunderstanding arises in your marriage. He or she is going to step in to solve the matter there and then before it escalates any further.

Finally, in order to avoid failure in the family and guarantee success for everyone, whenever you are blessed with children, although they are the most precious gift from God (Allah) consider the children to be liabilities and not assets, because your attitude towards them and their upbringing from the beginning will eventually determine their future, whether they will be instrumental in supporting your strengthism or not. However, if you nurture them properly and they become important assets, it is then children will be the strength to support your matrimonial home. Children from any marriage are metaphorical employees for the company and the strength of each employee is crucial to success for the welfare of any company.

From this chapter you have learned how to effectively attain success in many different ways: whether the theory of success is related to your private or public life, it is all included in the chapter. Although the concept of success is broad and complex, it means different things to different people. To me success means whenever you had attained satisfaction from something, you have succeeded. Success is not limited only to monetary and material gain; it is much broad and wider than that. You can come up with your own idea about what success means to you.

3: THE IMPORTANCE OF ROLE MODELS IN SOCIETY

No matter how much you love someone, if they fail to live up to your expectations, one day perhaps you might hate them. If you respect someone, but eventually that person behaves unethically or immorally, you will be massively disappointed with them. If you like somebody but that person is horrible to you, there is no doubt that you will be resentful of them. But when you are inspired by someone, and that inspiration becomes admiration and then aspiration, that person has become your role model. I called these people golden role models.

However, when such infatuation progresses much further and it subsequently engulfs your mind then the person is no longer just a role model to you: they become a mentor as well. My conversation in this chapter will focus on those two subjects: the role of a role model and the significance of a mentor.

As far back as the beginning of memory role models and mentors occur not only in human societies but also among primates. A role model not only gives purpose and courage for people to excel, but it also helps people to improve themselves socially and spiritually. While each person is struggling to make sense of the world, role models shape society to become more productive.

There are four main kinds of role models and I will give a practical example of each type. Each role model can go on to be a mentor. Let me start the conversation with the first category which is:

a) The classic role model

Classic role models to me are perfect and natural. They include prophets, messiahs, holy men and holy women. I consider them to be classic role models because they live their entire lives by setting a good example and inspiring people to become like them. Even though they are all human, they try to be perfect as possible; they make extreme sacrifices and all aspects of their lives are designed just to inspire people to live as purely as possible and as rightful as they command. As a Muslim, our first role model is the prophet Muhammad PBUH. He lived his life setting good examples, his spouses are the role models for our mothers, and his children and grandchildren are the role models to our sons and daughters. Every single Muslim is inspired by his noble course and actions; we want to follow the examples he set for us and try to live by them by all means necessary. The prophet Muhammad PBUH is a classic role model and also a mentor for Muslims.

The same example is true of other people who go by the books known as Abrahamic faiths. Each group of them follows the example set by their own prophet.

I list prophets, messiahs and holy people as classic role models because the unique position they occupy in the memories of people will never change. The prophet Muhammad will never cease to be the founder of Islam, neither will the prophet (Essa) Jesus ever cease to be the founder of Christianity. They, and many like them, will continue to be influential and inspiring for billions of people.

You might wonder why you have to follow the example set by them and live your life as purely as them, because they are no longer alive. Well, don't be confused, true classic role models will never cease to influence people, because the multitude of stories written about prophets and holy people are scattered in the pages of thousands of books and stored in millions of individual memories. Read their stories as much as possible, question religious scholars and take note what would work for you. You can use the examples that matter to you the most, and you can apply them to each aspect of your life. But it is crucial to bear in mind that, no matter how spiritual you are considered to be, following their example in today's society will not be easy.

For example, if you believe that the cause of trouble in the world is sexual desire and lust for women, and the story of Jesus inspired you to become celibate, this might not necessarily prevent you from committing sexual sins. If a Muslim thinks he can produce many children because of the inspiration of the prophet Muhammad's many spouses, looking after so many wives and children could create more trouble than he was bargaining for.

But you can take from your classic role models whatever you wish, and use it in modern society until you attain a pure life.

If you want to become a holy person, to attain a higher spiritual plane, you can learn a lot from the inspirational stories of holy men and women around the globe, both from the past and the present. Just choose someone who has captured your imagination, or perhaps you can choose one from your own community and let that person serve as your spiritual role model. A few years back, I did exactly that. While I was looking for more profound spiritual enlightenment, the amazing story that inspired me the most was the story of the 10th century Islamic scholar and holy man called Imam Muhammad Ghazali. I adopted him to be my spiritual mentor, and since then I try to follow his example. He is also my intellectual role model, thus he is my second classic role model.

b) The golden role model

I would divide this category into two sections. The first includes politicians, celebrities, professionals and royal personages. The second includes farmers, virtuous individuals, religious people and ordinary people.

Let's start the conversation first by assuming that you are a golden role model. The most satisfactory good feeling comes when people start imitating you and comparing their lives to your life, with admiration and willingness to follow your example. Everyone looks up to you and people from all walks of life consider you to be their role model; there would be no prouder moment for you. But I think it is worth pointing out that there is a clear distinction between following somebody's example and having a wild admiration of them.

You may be infatuated with someone's lifestyle, or perhaps their image captured your imagination, so they are really adorable to you, but despite all that you still don't still consider them to be a good role model for you. In the current political climate, you might say this of Donald Trump and Kim Jong-un; the duo are interesting characters but you might not be proud of their political philosophy. Michael Jackson and Amy Winehouse were very talented artists but you wouldn't be attracted to their lifestyle. Another point which is central to human advancement is that following a role model doesn't mean copying them or pretending to lead your life as they did, speak like them, talk like them or even change your name to theirs. It is all about thinking about their ideas and applying them to your life. Be inspired by their efforts, set as good an example as them and contribute towards society as they did.

No human beings are perfect. You can't find the perfect

role model but you can always strive to associate yourself with good people. For example, if you were inspired by Michael Jackson's talent as a musician, it wouldn't harm you to work as hard as Michael did; but you don't have to bleach your skin to look like a white man.

The different between classic role models and golden role models is this, you can pick and choose your own golden role model, but usually you are born to follow your classic role model.

You can pick your role model from powerful and popular politicians, or rich and famous celebrities, or influential and virtuous professionals, or glorious and wealthy royals. You can choose role models at any time of your life. For example, your role model in primary school might differ from your high school or university role model. Use the power of your imagination and ensure the role model is measured by merit and virtue, not merely from their bank balance or popularity.

If you want to become a politician, choose political role models. If you want become a professional choose a professional role model, etc. You are always free to change your role model. If you feel awkward about associating yourself with a particular individual, try someone else. Recently I switched my political role models to Marcus Garvey and Mahatma Gandhi, because I find their political philosophy very fascinating. These two gentlemen laid the foundation of peaceful revolution which seized power from colonial masters and gave full independence to many countries. If I decide to participate in any political process, I might consider using their political strategies. However, in the future this might change; I might replace their political ideology with another one.

Now let examine the second section. Often people don't

realise that there are many potential role models in our midst: they think that role models are always unique people. It's much broader than that. Role models can be farmers, virtuous people, religious people and even ordinary individuals. The lives of billions of people around the world are entirely dependent on farmers; it is not easy to get wealthy through farming, but farming provides meaningful life to many millions of men and women around the world and it prevent people from engaging in other activities, aspects of which might involve crimes. Consequently farmers are role models to many.

Virtuous and religious people are just as good a role model as everyone I previously mentioned. Can you imagine a society without people of virtue and excellent character? Even though they may not be rich, famous, powerful, or influential, they are gentle, humble, honest, kind and above all, they are trustworthy. Each of these virtues is an attribute of a role model who contributes to society and gives hope, peace, love, happiness, and tranquillity. Even an ordinary person can play this role very effectively and be a role model.

What happens if you have no golden role models

In developed countries where there are many role models, people are more inspirational and more creative than those in societies with fewer role models. For example, the United Kingdom and the Ivory Coast have equal opportunity to put their weight behind a football team. The United Kingdom has more professional football players than the Ivory Coast, and the quality of their professional football players are the same. However, the children of the United Kingdom have more advantage in football than the Ivory Coast, because the former have more role models in football than the latter.

Clever people want to measure their performance against their role models. Where there is need for improvement, role models help to motivate people and to follow the example set by them. Underdeveloped countries lack role models, hence the economic gap between them and developed countries is wide.

Use the power of your positive imagination and become your own role model. The successful black author Maya Angelou is her own role model. She used the power of her positive imagination and subsequently become the mother of many marvellous books. If you want to be as successful as Maya Angelou, here is what I learnt from her biography;

Just do right and be courageous. Love people as much as you can, laugh as loud as you can and be a blessing to someone. You are already talented, turn struggle to triumph but no matter what, learn to say no. Always do your best, and one day you will rise up.

This is fantastic advice, isn't it? You may not be interested in publishing a book, but you can still apply the virtues of Maya and become your own role model, as well as a role model for society. Your role model is doesn't have to have the same profession or hobby as you. Whoever inspires you to have that extra strength, which enhances your ambition, also can be a role model to you. For instance, the hard work of Beyoncé as a musician might inspire someone to become a firebrand Imam in a mosque or Pastor in a church. Equally, Barack Obama's public speaking skills could influence someone to become the most powerful lawyer in the courtroom.

Perhaps in the modern generation, the most unexpected role model was Nelson Mandela. Mandela was labelled as a terrorist by his opponents, but eventually he won the Nobel peace prize and subsequently became a revolutionary hero and an international role model, not only to black communities but all communities. Here is a flavour of his long walk to freedom:

Demand respect and prove them wrong, use your time wisely, don't worry about labels. Be humble, take a stand but don't be emotional, manage your emotions, speak with conviction and be willing to die for your cause.

If you hold firm to these 'Mandela virtues', even if you are from a remote corner of an African village or the highlands of South Asia, you can become anything you wish, and maybe unexpectedly someday you will become an international role model.

Again, if you are not familiar with the people I mention, search for their biographies and find out more information about them. That will be really essential to your own journey, so that one day, you can become your own story for the generations to come.

Having a role model in our midst means there is a sense of belonging in the community. It is possible that your role model may not even be a successful person, yet you can still associate your ideas with their ideas. If I can put this in to perspective, for instance, you might want to walk from Sydney to London barefoot, which no one has ever attempted. However, if one day you read in the newspaper that someone had unsuccessfully attempted to walk from London to New York City, undoubtedly you would be relieved, because that person would still give you a sense of belonging. All that you need to learn from this person is from their failure. Perhaps all you find out is that there are crazy people out there who think in exactly the same way as you!

In another scenario, let's say one of your classmates couldn't attract the attention of the most beautiful girl is the classroom; his failure might serve as sense of belonging for others who failed in a similar attempt. Associating yourself with people who fail might sound crazy, but what you get from them is the sense of belonging, which people usually get from their role models. You won't always get satisfaction from everything you do, and your role models don't have to always succeed.

If you are lucky enough to be a golden role model, your role is crucial for society. It does not only includes encouraging people to do what is right and avoid all that is wrong, but each aspect of your life will empower and inspire people, both physically and ethically. As a role model you don't necessarily have to tell people what to do, but you are dictating their behaviour by your actions.

I don't know of a society where the role of role models is codified or set in the stone, but having certain virtues would guarantee admiration of you. The following might serve to strengthen your appeal; appropriate dress code, physical discipline, impressive character, positive vocabulary and good behaviour. By contrast, being compulsive or aggressive won't help you achieve anything. Negative traits such as ruthlessness, lack of empathy, bad manners and swearing in public won't bring you any favours either.

Despite saying this, we are all humans; often when we are confronted with certain circumstances often we tend to ignore boundaries. But whether you consider yourself to be a role model or not, everyone ought to obey social norms, even if sometimes they might be at odds with our individual beliefs. With the current 24 hour news media putting everyone, and particularly role models, in the spotlight with tremendous scrutiny, massive expectation lies on the shoulders of our public figures, each of whom is a golden role model. Thus, while new values are occasionally introduced to society, the common responsibility which binds us together is the only key to shape the future and produce virtues which will continue to empower our role models.

If you are a student, your golden role model is your teacher. Apart from your parents and siblings the most important people for you are teachers. They are the most influential people around adults and children, thus they become role models for everyone. People don't only learn skills from teachers but also they learn their manners, behaviour and attitudes.

Imagine when you wake up in the morning, and after breakfast it's time to go to school; but it is part of the school rule for every student to look smart. You put your school uniform on but it looks scruffy from the previous day. Despite this you don't care about how you look, you don't care about disciplinary action or a possible warning letter to your parents, you just go to school. The teacher is not impressed and he decides to send you home. Are you a role model to your fellow students? I don't think so.

Will you make the same mistake again? If you're smart, you won't. If it happens to be your classmate who is behaving in such a way, would you ever consider them a role model? Not really. If you noticed such behaviour in your favourite teacher, would he ever become your role model?

Generally people who are always dress smart and look professional command respect in society and eventually they become role models.

Religious leaders play a crucial role in society. They are intermediaries between people and God. Being an Imam is a most prestigious job for Muslim men and being the wife of an Imam is the most attractive position for a Muslim women. The same is true in Christian society. They follow certain strict guidelines on how to conduct themselves. They are provide moral guidance and also they are the custodians of almost all human values including symbolising the truth here on earth while encouraging people to have forgiveness, to give them hope, to teach them the virtue of being honest, to teach them how to show kindness to others, to make them understand the benefit of trustworthiness, and build the bridge of reconciliation between people. This is the basis of human values and we should endeavour to learn it. In my opinion, people lacking in some of these attributes will honestly struggle to be role models to anyone. Role models should have these attributes from birth.

The integrity of doctors, nurses, and men and women in uniform inspire millions, who look up to these people and want to become like them. Golden role models encourage many children from different backgrounds to follow in their footsteps, dream big and become a similar role model for future generations.

You might not be attracted to the material gains of people in these professions but the value they add to the community is extremely important. Your role model doesn't have to be a rich person, it can be anyone who sets a good example in the community. An honest security guard might be a potential role model for you. Most people believe that role models are people who only have wealth and influence. Some people even think role models are limited to a certain race and particular colour, but I hope you can see that the situation is completely different.
Let's slightly change direction to explore the background of some sportspeople. Yaya Touré comes from a very humble family background, with almost no family connection to international football. He is a super-talented football player with magnificent disciplined behaviour who

reached the international stage, but his story of success started from humble beginnings with a dream to become someone special. His success has nothing to do with his family's wealth, fame or popularity. We can see from this that if you have some discipline, and you are humble with good behaviour, this is a way to become a superman. The same is true for Didier Drogba, who came from the same country as Touré and had a similar humble story. However, Drogba spent the best part of his early life in France which had exposed him a little bit more to wealth and fame, but right from the beginning the duo faced similar challenges of low public expectation, lack of significant family connections, lack of adequate financial support and no role models at their disposal. Despite all this, the duo's self-discipline, dedication and conviction made them who they are today.

Let me put the success stories of Yaya Touré and Didier Drogba into perspective for the benefit to those who are not familiar with Africa. The negative Image of Africa which is always displayed by the media, particularly in the area of youth development is very hopeless. Yet the stories of people like Drogba and Touré will significantly help to improve that image. Probably you are familiar with the images of malnourished African children in charity adverts appealing for funds on television, and the stories of war, corruption, internal conflict, crime and much more. The children of Africa are the symbols of hunger and disease. The youth are the symbols of drug abuse and human trafficking. The elders are the symbols of illiteracy and conflict. Behind all this is manipulation of dependency and receiving foreign aid. In my opinion, these negative symbols send the signal to the world that there is no hope for African children and there is no legacy for African leaders.

We must collectively replace these negative symbols of

failure with three positive steps of hope and resilience.

1. provide quality education for every child, which will eventually prepare them to become better youths
2. create job opportunities for youths which would prepare them to become the best role models.
3. recognise the contribution of African leaders in showing the world that they left a remarkable legacy.

If we don't do this, people will have the following doubts. How can you encourage someone to enrol in university to have an opportunity for a better life and become financially independent, if his role models got rich through selling drugs during the day and stealing people's property at night? How can Africa attain economic superpower status and become self-reliant if the children are the symbols of hopelessness and grief, their youths are the symbols of crime, and their leaders are the symbols of corruption and conflict. And how could you encourage a young girl to respect her body and take her education seriously, if her role models are mistresses of foreign tourists and her mother is a victim of domestic violence? Critical thinking by using the power of positive imagination to diagnose Africa's long-term illness is long overdue.

The negative image which I highlighted is how people see Africa. If someone else other than me raises these issues, they might be perceived as racist or prejudiced against black people. But honestly I am stating a fact, not expressing mere opinion. The social narrative controlled by invincible super powers and used by the media is what dictates public opinion. The media usually promotes the views of multinational institutions operating behind the scenes. Thus, the role models the media show to the public are usually promote certain marketing agendas to entice the public's imagination. Role models created by the media and shown on TV are for mere propaganda reasons in order to suit their narrative, brainwash innocent people and feed a certain market interest.

We genuinely understand that the abhorrent gang-related violence which plagues the black community in the UK, particularly in Greater London, is horrible. However, whenever such appalling crimes occur, the media frequently point the finger at social breakdown and lack of role models prevalent not only in black communities, but in modern society as a whole.

But I think it is just part of a big picture. There are many other reasons: lack of quality education for black youths, stereotypical crime profiling, selective justice towards poor and disadvantaged people, and lack of job opportunities for all. In my opinion, the modern public perception of role models shown on TV every day is a distorted version profoundly contrary to the real role models people deserve. Such representation of false role models is decreasing the confidence and self-esteem of young people.

As result, the young generation are under too much pressure to look precisely like those images often shown on TV. Such a notion of role models greatly affects young women working in the modelling business, as well as art and sports institutions. Please don't take my assertion out of context; of course it's not wrong for people to seek their role models in the media, but it should not be allowed for commercials to trick young women into believing that the seemingly malnourished girls seen on TV are the best role models, or teaching black women to assume that bleaching their skin to look more white is the best approach.

As I said before, Didier Drogba, Yaya Touré and the like

are very positive role models. Use the power of your positive imagination to understand that the best role models often come from very humble beginnings; you don't certainly need an alien from the space to teach you who are the best role models for you. If you distil the virtues and attributes I have talked about you can choose your own golden role models wisely and perhaps they will subsequently become your mentors.

c) The basic role model

Your mother, father and siblings are the first basic role model for you. This is a simpler concept that those above, because basic role models are not only known to you, but you are very familiar with them and mingling with them every single day.

But before we start the conversation let me first ask you some straightforward questions. When did you become aware that your name is your name? And do you still remember the first person who taught you about the value of your mum and dad? Who taught you the following - how to eat your dinner, how to say your mum and dad's names, how to use the bathroom, how to seek help from your family and friends, how to notice danger in public, how to avoid bad people, how to approach society in general, how to respect human beings, how to do your homework, how to appreciate people's generosity, how to clean yourself, how to treat your siblings, extended family and relatives, and finally how to appreciate God blessing?
Have you been puzzled by these questions? I can vividly imagine you nodding your head slightly from the right to the left while trying so hard to get a response from your imagination. Rather than feeling peculiar about it, why can't you just say honestly "Yaya, I can't really recall the first person who unleashed human civilisation on me, however, I think I learnt these manners from my basic role

models, my mum and dad." And you would be right.

My encounters with basic role models

Your family gradually introduce you to the idea of basic role models. Usually they would introduce to you to people from your neighbourhood and members of your extended family. When I was a young boy, my mum set certain strict codified examples which I was obliged to adhere to no matter what. In addition to that, both my grandma and grandpa set their own standard rules. I was strictly encouraged to follow them too. Even though I struggled little bit from the start to understand the importunacy of adopting such complicated social rules and regulations, guess what, amazingly beyond any reasonable doubt in the end I had effectively mastered every single aspect of those rules until I became a basic role model for my younger siblings.

Such customs are prevalent in every society. I was not alone learning those basic rules. Due to my position as the eldest boy in the family, I had to introduce the same values to the next generation.

Philosophically, no human beings are born with culture, religion or knowledge. These virtues are usually introduced to them by their basic role models right from the beginning. However, they are naturally equipped with basic intelligence, which is why during the infancy they cry when they feel hungry, they smile when they feel happy and they sleep when they feel tired. Apart from this natural intelligence, they learn every single behaviour, social norms, attitudes, and character from their basic role models. Therefore, as a basic role model it is absolutely essential to prepare yourself in advance before you visit parenthood. Well behaved children often have good basic role models and children with bad habits usually learn them from bad basic role models. When you encounter naked children in the street and you engage them in conversation as to why they feel comfortable nakedly wandering out there, the usual response is the same; such behaviour is normal at home. When you interrogate children who beg from strangers, they would not hesitate to point the finger of blame at their basic role models. I believe that no human being is born to be a bad person. Whatever made them bad is introduced to them by their basic role models (perhaps occasionally it might be natural causes such as mental problems).

As a basic role model you are the custodians of social norms, whereas the aspiration behind each part of your behaviour, whether it is related to the common cultural practice, or traditional rules and manners, or religious beliefs and rituals, is the key component which influences children's behaviour, manners, and attitude towards life in general. These common social sciences which children learn from their basic role models will effectively determine their future, good or bad.

In modern society, through the advance of technology and mass media, people can be inspired by basic role models without even physically contacting them. I can still recall the late 1980s when people in our village had first encountered television images. The well-known Hong Kong martial artist actor Bruce Lee captured our imagination. Not only the children, but every young adult in the village was mesmerised by him. Due to his skilful entertaining abilities as a martial artist, every single young boy in the village tried to master martial arts, with such wild admiration he became like a cult. There was no story in the village which was more important than his. After a few of months, most boys in our group had assumed the nickname 'Bruce Lee'. Children in the village would engage in the most brutal and dangerous acts by imitating him as best they could, without realising that what he did on screen was not real, it was just a film. Yet, the innocent minds of young villagers were captivated by this new invincible hero. He was a basic role model controlling our emotion and influencing our behaviour from thousands of miles away.

I am amazed that no one was injured when we tried to imitate Bruce Lee. But I do remember the possible negative impact of such dangerous action films. It introduced violent behaviour to children and the temptation of using abusive language. At that time we could not really understand the language he used, but we used our imagination and pretended as if we really understand what they were talking about. At one point some boys who were learning English at primary school tried to translate what Bruce Lee and his co-stars were saying.

We can see that basic role models for children are not limited only to those who share the same environment as them, but it also includes the images and information available to them as well. The information is as effective as physical contact with someone. Often basic role models create destructive avenues for their children without realising it. In reality what people learn from each other has more impact on their lives than what they learn from books. There are strict guidelines and tough punishment for those who expose children to the wrong materials. Films, TV ads, and internet are all included. If governments don't intervene, parental failure to protect children from this undesirable media would result in catastrophic consequences for the children. In our day, we didn't have a clue about the minimum age requirement to watch a martial arts film. Our basic role models didn't understand the significance of films which were dangerous for children. Unknowingly we were exposed to unpleasant ideas polluting our minds with possible psychological traumas. To this day I don't watch such aggressive media and I believe children shouldn't either.

But introducing educational materials to children, such as TV documentaries, the history of important people, stories from conventional wisdom, and quotes from local intellectuals, as well as literature in a foreign language is crucial to nurture future minds. This is much more effective than entertaining them with action films and violent games.

For a basic role model the most powerful strategy to use in order to convince your disciples is to display your internal qualities and demonstrate those in your action; in reality this is what actually inspires good people to follow your command.

In my previous book Marriage and Society, I extensively outlined some of the major challenges people encounter particularly when they look for role models and mentors to inspire them. These challenges include lack of information about potential role models. Because you often have to pay for access to genuine stories about good basic role models and mentors, it is often easy to accumulate outdated ideas from free information which has no value for modern society whatsoever. Our addiction for the internet hinders people's ability to find the truth. The culture of high dependency on digital intelligence has become the norm. With addiction comes a slow journey to the end of quality human interaction. The obsessive behaviour prevalent in each society by adhering to rules set by famous and rich people, including subscribing to negative values invented by unscrupulous celebrities has trapped innocent people. The perfect example of this is the culture of online pornography and consumption of sexual enhancement medication which greatly influences modern adult sex life.

Consumers subscribing to pornography might become addicted. It is not recognised that such materials are harmful to emotional health and psychological wellbeing. Consuming pornography just to promote sexual power is harmful to mental health, particularly for men. It also weakens the moral strength of married couples to stay loyal to one another because it gives a false expectation of what a sexual relationship should be.

More importantly, sexual exploitation of women caught up in pornography is so degrading. Pornography only portrays women as sexual objects, places little value on their humanity and frequently promotes misogyny.

I published this finding in my book Marriage and Society in 2014. Two year later, in August 2016 there was an article published in the UK Daily Mail newspaper with the headline "Online porn harms young men's health." The content of this article had proved my point. The article was written by Dr. Angela Gregory, a psycho-sexual therapist. She pointed out the correlation between online pornography and erectile dysfunction, which is increasingly experienced by young men. The connection between the two is too serious to ignore. It is a moral obligation for authors, politicians, celebrities and doctors to reach out to young generation wherever and whenever it is possible in order to tackle this serious issue. Online misinformation and the paradoxical attitude of parents undermines good behaviour in the younger generation, hence there is always a need for good role models to help them distinguish good from bad.

Another reason we need basic role models is the great emotional attachment to rich and famous people. Almost everyone in modern society, especially young people, has some sort of idol in the entertainment business, whether it is sport, music, acting or modelling.

Let me use footballers as an example. If you are a Manchester United football fan, you might say every member of the team is an idol and role model. You don't care about their character or personality; all that you care is that they must win every match with teamwork and team spirit. If you're young, everything they do influences your behaviour, you follow them through thick and thin and whenever they win a game, you celebrate with them. Whenever they lose a game, you are devastated. Each season you buy a new football strip. You even have the same hair cut as one of the players! Despite this, the club doesn't know you, and it doesn't really care about your feelings.

You may ask yourself, why am I wasting my energy supporting a team which doesn't even know me? Here is a simple answer - "feeling is more powerful than touching" - every human being is a slave to his or her own feelings. It is purely due to such adulation, you can easily be misled by the behaviour of golden role models.

It is absolutely important for entertainment role models to recognise that every aspect of their life can massively influence people's behaviour.

It is essential to scrutinise certain aspects of your role model's life, particularly the areas that matter to you dearly. It is a bit like an encounter with a romantic book: when you find it interesting you tend to read it from cover to cover in order to familiarise yourself with it as much as possible and take from it the things which captivated your imagination. However, such intense curiosity about your role model doesn't give you any warrant to cross the boundaries by invading someone's private life. You don't have to copy them and live your life exactly as them, but you can emulate them by living the good examples set by them. No matter how successful someone seems to be, it is crucial for you to learn from their failures as well as learn how they overcome challenges.

I would like to share an interesting experience from April 2016 when I was in Sydney, Australia, at the Key Person of Influence annual conference. During the conference, there was a presentation in which five contestants were chosen from the audience to give a speech in order to persuade the judges, who were acting as potential clients, to invest with them. The speech delivered by the first two contestants wasn't persuasive enough to sway the opinion of anyone in the gathering. They didn't capture the judges' imagination or the attention of audience. They didn't have enough confidence, or a serious business investment plan. The duo couldn't demonstrate the professional skills which would attract the attention of potential investors. However, after the break, the last three contestants effectively became basic role models for each other. They had already learnt from the failure of the previous two contestants; each of the three visibly displayed confidence in their speech, and showed the public that they could be trusted to invest funds. Each one appeared calm and serious, and impressed the audience. They swayed the public opinion their way, and persuaded the judges to make rational decisions.

Those five contestants were not facing real life investors, but they had indicated from their presentations that they could be useful basic role models for one another. All that it takes to pursue imagination and conquer the world is your conviction and your willingness to learn from those who had conquered the world before you. Don't just learn from the success of your role models, but also learn from their failure and emulate their expertise as effectively as you can. To conquer the world, you don't need a bachelor degree in politics or a masters degree in economics or a PhD in science from Cambridge Uni. All that you need to conquer the world is your profound conviction and your determination.

Remember, in the 15th century, Christopher Columbus and his companions who discovered the new world known today as America, were not sophisticated people who had modern tools and technology. Unbelievably they had accomplished a monumental achievement and history continues to honour their legacy. If you cultivate the culture of hard teamwork and team spirit, you can achieve similar goals through sheer dedication and firmly holding on to your values.

The criteria for being a basic role model are not set in the stone, they evolve accordingly, and you ought to evolve along with them. The more you grow up emotionally and spiritually, the more you will need to find the role models to inspire you to the next level. Initially the basic role models for most people are siblings, parents, members of your close and extended families, and neighbours. However, when you change environment, like when you go to school, your aspirations usually change, along with your self-esteem. Your friends and school teachers might become your role models. You might be a role model for someone else. But no matter how you choose them, the most effective basic role models come from the group of people which really inspires society, particularly in the areas of education, economy, healthcare and social welfare. These are role models which you might genuinely feel passionate about.

Music has the influence of a basic role model

You may be surprised to learn that, apart from consuming illicit drugs like heroin, cocaine, alcohol, and cannabis; nothing is more harmful in intoxicating the human mind or polluting the imagination than music.

The phenomenal pleasure people gain through listening to music is beyond human comprehension. Because music is emotionally and naturally designed to cause the brain to function in a certain way, it takes you on a journey to a different atmosphere, or perhaps if I am going to be honest let's say it totally takes you to a different planet.

Even without physical interaction with the singer, the magical power of the mixture of sweet melody and rhythm is enough to inspire people to do right or wrong. Music has the role of a basic role model in society. I think it is essential to highlight how different cultures view the role of music in the society.

The concept of music in the Gulf countries

Ultra-conservative religious movements e.g. Wahhabis and their sympathisers in the Middle East, especially the Gulf countries in the Arabian peninsula, have strongly condemned music. According to their religious doctrine, using musical instruments is equal to using weapons of mass destruction.

They believe music is the instrument of Satan. Such an attitude towards music was not widespread in the Muslim world in the past. However, with the growing muscle of the Saudi Wahhabism movement around the globe, boosted by oil revenue, this attitude towards music is increasingly becoming prevalent in other Muslim societies. Ultra-conservative scholars and radical clerics are tirelessly campaigning to totally ban music from Muslim society, without any adequate evidence to support their argument. The main reason usually cited by them is that, during Jahiliyyah, commonly known as the period of ignorance, pagan worshippers in Arabia used the music to entertain their idols, and in the early days of Islam, the Kufaru of Arabia (non-believers) used music to mock the religion of early Muslims.

The logic behind this argument sounds totally alien to many societies. It won't convince someone from South Asia, Africa, Australia and Europe, where ancient people used music to comfort themselves and celebrate the glory of life.

Perhaps an argument against music using similar logic from the modern world might sound like this: it is akin to the families of the victims' of 9-11 campaigning to ban people from using aeroplanes as methods of travel because aeroplanes were used as missiles to slaughter their loved ones. We understand from the rational perspective that the purpose of building aeroplanes is not to use them as weapons. However, on 9-11, a group of terrorists did exactly that.

The new killer method for terrorists is using heavy vehicles to disrupt and destroy large crowds; however, so far there is no campaign to ban peoples from using those vehicles.
Equally, campaigning to totally prevent people from listening to all music is not enough to tackle antisocial behaviour as I have discussed above. Due to the significant role which music plays for most people we ought to carefully examine exactly which types of music are dangerous. Although I never support the position of anti-music movements, I am not attempting to dismiss their argument entirely, because we must recognise that there are certain aspects of music which could be lethal for our youths, capitalising on their ignorance of certain areas. Therefore in this discussion, I will suggest how to approach music in general, as well as how to deal with people working in the music industry, but before that I would like to discuss how music influences and inspires people in Africa, Asia and Western societies.

The role of music in Africa

In almost every corner of Africa, music is a significant part of people's culture and tradition. In this chaotic world, from the beginning of human history, when confronted with death and its misery, mankind struggles to make sense of its own existence. In order for humankind to actually comprehend the meaning of life, a spiritual connection between them and a deity is crucial. Before outside contact, people in ancient Africa use music to achieve this; as a result music became a role model to Africans. Indigenous people in Africa used music to celebrate the glory of life and sought comfort from its melody and rhythm, especially during periods of sadness, misery, trials and tribulations. In both ancient and modern Africa, music is used in a variety of entertainment areas. The sight and sound of music has a profound impact by inspiring people psychologically, emotionally and spiritually and it is instrumental in manifesting good behaviour in people. The origin of music in Africa is oral, therefore different cultures give different accounts based on their environment. However, in West Africa where I was born, music had its own stories. However, I will limit my discussion to the type of music which inspires people to become a role model.

The true history of Africa is contextual and not easily understood due to varying accounts told by different ethnic groups, usually narrated in a way which is most suitable to serve their social and political interests. When Africa came into contact with foreign influence e.g. white Christians and Arab Muslims, the ancient history of the continent was further shrouded in mystery, as new values took hold.

But despite all that music is a big part of African history. The majority, maybe 90%, has been narrated by traditional music players or praise singers, known as griot in West Africa. Even the remaining 10% written in books has a root in those traditional story tellers.

The stories told by traditional musicians continue to inspire millions of people from all walks of life. It is a common occurrence in African culture that when someone wanted to inspire others to do right and avoid wrong he or she would organise a music ceremony with a famous intellectual griot who would entertaining peoples while narrating the inspirational stories of legendary Africans who made a significant different to society, in order to encourage young people to emulate them. Music is frequently use as a basic role model to remind people of the ultimate sacrifice of their ancestors, particularly during the medieval period when they were confronted with civil war, foreign aggression, disease and drought.

Until very recently most people in Africa sought role models only through their interaction with musicians. Through the sound of music they learned the heroic stories of ancient legendary African rulers. Music helped to foster peace, love and harmony between different ethnic groups. People used music to comfort each other and musicians aided the spread of information. Through music, people gained psychological wisdom and emotional wellbeing which strengthened their hope and added meaning to their life.

Music is also used as metaphorical medicine to diagnose the psychological trauma caused by social anxiety. Without consultation with traditional musicians who are well versed in the oral history of Africa, you will struggle to gather authentic information about the history of African nobles, the influence of their celebrities, the wisdom of their religious scholars, the techniques use in agriculture, the secret behind African magic, the medicine from African science, the quality of African astrology, and the social norms of Africa.

Basically to cut a long story short, musicians are the custodians of the intellectual bounty of African cosmology, primitive human history and all social norms. Consequently, music has a profound impact on the Sunni Islamic branch of Sufism, which is one of the spiritual movements from mainstream Sunni Islam, especially in the West and North Africa. People practising Sufism in those regions often use music to enhance their spiritual imagination while meditating and contemplating about life and the afterlife. Thus music is not only socially significant but also spiritually significant. Apart from physical interaction, music is the most effective tool to influence and inspire people's behaviour, particularly that of young people. The melody and lyrics are among the most efficient energies to enlighten the public mood whenever there is misery or grief. The evangelist Christians in Africa and Europe also frequently use music in church to entertain their followers as well as celebrate the life of Jesus.

In rural East and Central Africa, during the night, often when a child cries, adults would usually beat drums as comfort, to entertain the children while narrating beautiful. As a result most children grow up learning about love and affection through the sound and lyrics of music.

Hence by using the power of your positive imagination you can see that music is a big asset which helps to empower young people, and its role in the society is equal to a basic role model. I noticed one major phenomenon, particularly in Africa, which is this; whenever you read a story from a book you won't get much attention, but music is guaranteed to attract the attention of everyone.

Removing music from society would not only remove melody and rhythm from society but it is would also remove large chunk of human values and a significant amount of intellectual material. Maybe this is a subjective opinion, particularly for the ultra-conservative movement, but in my humble opinion, it is extremely important to give it serious consideration.

The role of music in the East and the West

In Europe, Asia, Australia and elsewhere, music has a similar effect to that of societies like Africa and Asia. Its role in society is equal to a basic role model , with similar power to inspire and influence public behaviour and attitude.

For example in Europe, music is crucial in people's romantic lives, as well as encouraging children to become artists. The reality TV show Britain's Got Talent originated in the United Kingdom and subsequently became the most influential reality television program in the world. This invincible basic role model has attracted millions of exuberant youths around the world and inspired them with dedication and determination to try to become international superstars. In modern society the melody and lyrics of music is the only magic which has the power to generate such an influence on young people. I will discuss some possible side effects from the instruments of music, but for now, I would emphasise once again, the overwhelming numbers of reality TV shows in the US and UK have profoundly transformed thousands of lives especially those from poor and disadvantaged family backgrounds.

Overnight people became more creative as well as more innovative. From using music instruments, similar progress has been made by young people in India, Japan, Brazil and the Western hemisphere. For instance, from the 15th to the18th century, during the several hundred years of trans-Atlantic slave trade, black Africans were forcefully taken to North, South, and Central America. These slaves used the instrument of music for spiritual comfort as well as entertainment. The abhorrence of slavery compelled the descendants of African slaves living in these regions to use music and musicians as the main source of their role models.

But now let's hear the counter argument about the possible dangers music could introduce to society.

The negative aspect of music

Let me start with our own experience. After gaining independence in the 1960s, black men used many different ways to entertain themselves. However, in the 1970s, 80s and 90s West Africa had gone through many social as well as cultural transformations. Tourism from the West and music from Caribbean had played a big part in this. Music directly impacted social and cultural transformation. For example, rock and reggae music from Jamaica composed by superstars like Bob Marley, Ijahman, Burning Spear and many others introduced negative habits like smoking cannabis and wrong attitudes such as resentment towards authorities. Not many people fully understood the language and slang used by musicians but the melody sound and rhythm and the vocal rhetoric were enough to create antisocial behaviour.

At the time there were no images on video to show what these reggae superstars looked like and no books to explain how they lived their lives; but people still used their imagination and visualised through the only images available to them on the dust jacket of cassette tapes. Reggae music encouraged people to adopt a reggae life style. Gradually young men started to look rough, men wore dreadlocks and openly smoked cannabis; a Rastafarian lifestyle became attractive to West African youths. It wasn't too long before harder drugs followed. Later on West Africa became a centre for Caribbean and American music, plus music from other parts of East, South and Central Africa. Music from each of these regions came with its own culture which challenged that of Africa. Before this happened, many of those influences were alien to West Africa. There is no doubt that, each of these influences contributed towards damaging society.

We need to discuss the best options to create basic role models from music, and also look for suitable types of music. It would take too long to list all the different types of music, so in this summary I will highlight the most influential music which is a basic role model for society and serves as an inspirational tool for youths.

I would divide music in to four categories. Each category consist four types of music with similar effects on society.

1: Reggae, Rap, Rock and R&B. The feelings people get from this music might inspire and influence young people to become anti-authority, exacerbate domestic and gang related violence and motivate them to take drugs. The logic behind my theory is that; most musicians belong to this category of music I had stated above usually don't have a high regard for authorities and often they encourage people to adopt similar behaviour.

2: Pop, Classical, Jazz and Country. The feelings people get from this music might inspire and influence young people to become involve more in politics, romantic life, and control their behaviour and alcohol consumption.

3: Solo music, traditional African music, Indian music and

opera. The feelings people get from this music might inspire and influence young people to become rulers, having a desire for glory, love of wealth and becoming more famous, but encourages people to exaggerate their abilities, as well as becoming greedy.

4: Poetry, religious music, military music, and soukous. The feelings people get from this music often remind people of internal and external pride, aiming to be more honourable and kind to people, encouraging spiritualism, a reflection on the past, contemplation of the personal circumstances as well as bravery in general. Even though this music has negative attributes, it is usually harmless.

However, here is my advice: when it comes to listening to the music in general, different people get different vibes from it. It is almost impossible to generalise the effect on everyone. Yet you cannot dispute that the impact of listening to music influences people's behaviour, whether good or bad, because music is equal to the role of a basic role model in society.

Let's have an example of sensational feelings produced by just listening to the music. In the summer of 2016, while I was visiting Brunei Darussalam, one Saturday afternoon I was sightseeing near the Sultan's presidential palace. While jogging, I had my headphones on listening to Resala on You Tube. Resala is Arabic traditional music which is the soundtrack of films which celebrate the life of the prophet Muhammad and his companions during the early days of their struggle in Arabia to establish Islam. The film shows 7th century Arabia and the hardship early Muslims endured at the hands of their pagan opponents. Resala music is one of my favourites, but that particular day in Brunei was a very special moment for me, because the sensational magic feelings which travelled through my soul from the lyrics and the sound of the music boosted my imagination with massive excitement, as if I owned the whole country of Brunei.

I had visions while I listened to that Resala music and I saw my ideas conquer the world. Such a moment is a familiar one for everybody who listens to music, isn't it? Often the magical power of music instruments creates unrealistic expectations or visions which are beyond imagination. Although most people have the mental capacity to manage their emotion, and contain their desire, occasionally music is like a drug. It has the power to dramatically influence people's behaviour and it isn't long before you notice a change in their attitudes.

d) Bad role models

Even though bad role models have no good attributes, I think we should discuss them for a while. The three types of role models above (classic, golden and basic) are actually relevant to an understanding of bad role models.

Bad role models possess the exact opposite attitudes to the three good roles models. For an example, when I discussed how to emulate the spiritual attitudes of a classic role model, whenever you encounter someone doing the exact opposite, he or she is a bad role model for you. I discussed attributes of the golden role model as peoples who like helping the poor and looking after the sick - whenever you encounter someone doing the opposite to this please realise that they are a bad role model for you. I discussed the good attributes of basic role models, particularly peoples who have the ability to inspire others - whenever you encounter somebody with opposite attributes, know that the person is a bad role model for you. Basically whoever sets a bad example in society is a bad role model. We have to strive and learn to understand how good people became good people so that we can emulate their actions, as well research to determine how bad people became bad people so that we can avoid their paths and collectively concentrate on inspiring peoples through our actions, until everyone becomes a good role model for society.

Critical analysis

Use your imagination to critically analyse public perception before being judgmental or jumping to a conclusion and determining people's fate. In this section I am attempting to analyse the circumstances which put a massive cloud over role models, which makes people think they are bad role models while in reality they are not. Occasionally culture can play a significant role in this.

Public consumption of alcohol in Islamic countries is mostly illegal, thus if you drink alcohol in such a society you will be labelled as a bad role model; whereas in the other societies, such behaviour is acceptable. Hence it is extremely important to take culture, religion and social norms into account before being judgmental and calling someone a bad role model. Additionally, committing one terrible mistake is not enough to disqualify somebody from being a good role model.

I am going to give an example, however, but I am not going to mention any names because often people do things they might regret. Role models are no exception to this. Therefore the story I will share with you is slightly vague but true. Here we go; a very famous talented artist in the west participated in sexual intercourse while filming with multiple guys, eventually the episode became pornographic. In the commotion, she was totally naked while having sex with fellow participants. Although the movie in question is no longer widely in circulation but her story and image remain in our imagination. Despite all that, she is very popular and even more talented than before. She is a wife, mother and role model to many people. Is such impulsive behaviour enough to brand someone a bad role model?

Here is my take on this; even though I am not supportive of what she did in the past, I don't think a single mistake means it is fair to brand someone as a bad role model. What we have to understand is no matter how famous someone is or how many titles they have, people have desires which they need to fulfil. Individualism, which I call the 'me' factor, is a very powerful impulse. Everyone has a dark corner in their soul which needs fulfilment. Often such fulfilments go un-noticed but occasionally they will come to light. Celebrities, politicians, community leaders, religious scholars, ruling elites, holy men and holy women are just normal people, they have their own little 'me' factors which need fulfilment, and that is not enough for people to disqualify them from being a good role models. All that we need to do is to keep our 'me' factor within social boundaries.

Perhaps currently the most famous and most respected woman in the world is the Queen of the United Kingdom but even she has her own 'me' factors. Every human is a sinner, consequently it is not morally right to constantly keep monitoring the behaviour of role models and spying on their private lives.

In 2016 in Europe a Champions League football player was jailed for sexually grooming a 15 year old girl. The guy in question is a very talented footballer, inspiring many young children. However, using his 'me' factor in a wrong way landed him in a most unpleasant place with profound regret. Is this massive error of judgment enough to strip him the title of a good role model and earn him the title of bad role model? Well in my opinion, not really. Although such appalling behaviour is not acceptable in any civilised society, but if God can forgive people when they have regretted their sins then how come humans cannot forgive?

No human being seeks to emulate such appalling behaviour of any role model, but we can emulate other aspects of their lives, particularly areas where they have contributed immensely to society and be prepared to forgive them whenever they had repented. In relation to this gentleman, he paid a heavy price for wrongfully fulfilling his 'me' factor, therefore I don't consider him a bad role model now. However, he ought to make sure a similar error is not repeated.

If you put yourself in their shoes, perhaps you will come to realise after all is not our business to constantly be judgmental of people's 'me' factors.

Constructive criticism might be used as a deterrent to ensure potential role models are deterred from abusing people by using their popularity to take advantage of weak and venerable peoples. Because in private celebrities wouldn't consider themselves as such. They are just ordinary people like as you and me, sometimes sensitive, emotional, with desires for pleasure. Thus they have every right to fulfil their human obligations within social and cultural boundaries, but every now and again they drop their guard and something else takes control.

For an example very recently a famous footballer was caught drunk driving: the story was all over the media. Apart from several times when he was caught committing the same offense, he is a very well behaved guy. Despite this, people now begin to consider his reckless behaviour the action of bad role model, due to nothing other than silly mistakes.

As I said before making mistakes infrequently is acceptable but if you make mistakes often you are considered a fool. Before we quickly jump to a conclusion to throw somebody in the rubbish bin, we have to weigh the burden of their attitudes in society against the qualities of their actions and the contribution they are making to communities; whatever weighs more, then we go along with that. Even if the role model had served a prison term or been convicted several times, as long as they are ready to reform, we should be ready to give them a second chance. We can make an exception for rape, murder, theft, kidnapping, and cannibalism. What is considering a serious crime in the West might be normal in the East. For instance "One man's terrorist is another man's freedom fighter".

Here's an interesting question: do we need bad role models in society?

I am not sure whether this question is an intelligent one or one that merely sparks a debate. Perhaps you can use the power of your positive imagination to answer it, but I will mention the following examples; the legendary story of Robin Hood in Europe, the history of Pablo Escobar, a drug cartel boss in Columbia, and Muammar Gaddafi, the former ruler of Libya. These characters amazingly captured people's imagination, and influenced and inspired millions around the world. Even though they were branded as criminals, no one can deny the huge contribution they made to their community by looking after the poor. Thus many people would want to become a 'bad' role model like them. Again culture, tradition, and religion is crucial to this discussion. The traditional position of religion is that we ought to do only good and avoid all which is bad. But are we truly capable of inspiring each individual to become a good role model only? I don't think we are. How do we handle people who are perceived as bad role models but do good?

Now let's determine how different cultures deal with the concept of bad role models.

Drug cartels from South and Central America and the Caribbean obtain their fortune through operating criminal enterprises. But they can undertake philanthropic activities such as providing education or affordable healthcare for disadvantaged families and in some cases they even provide weekly wages to prominent members of the society. They do good, but they are 'bad' role models. People shouldn't emulate the bad things they do, but the good things. So strangely, there can be a need for these 'bad' role models.

I read a book published by someone who used to work as escort and she stated in her book that 'In Europe, women seek wealth by operating brothels and providing escort services. People sell sex as prostitutes, young mothers work in massage parlours and offer adult entertainment services to the public.' As bad role models, they can get rich through tax evasion or illegally claiming public funds. Amazingly such people gradually climb the ladder to become prominent members of society taking part in charity fundraising events, participating in community services, and featuring in reality TV shows hosted by superstars.

Most people in Europe wouldn't seek their fortune by such means, however, the service they render to the public in the form of charity and entertainment increases popular demand for such bad role models to exist; a similar attitude in Asia, particularly in the Middle East, would be an invitation for the angel of death to knock on your door. But in the Middle East and South Asia, vulnerable people are often brainwashed, intimidated and blackmailed into hard labour in slave-like conditions. Usually the perpetrators are hardened criminals but due to the essential services they offer like giving food, medicine, and clothes to the poor and needy, society cannot afford to entirely remove them.

In Africa access to easy cash from sex tourism, human and drug trafficking, corruption and political dictatorship has benefitted many people in society. Frequently criminals who got rich in this way give back to the community by building roads, hospitals, schools, health centres, and mosques. Young girls working in sex tourist industries do it to make ends meet for their families.

But many of the African drug and human traffickers, and dictators have become rich through criminal syndicates. They are bad role models but they are helping communities by supporting their projects. Fortunately most youths do not emulate their criminal actions but their profound generosity hugely inspires many. Even though the general public is aware of the nitty-gritty behind such leaders, often they revere them.

I think by now you get the idea. We seek not to become a bad role model but they continue to exist and it is up to society to work out how to deal with them. Most people earning a living through criminal means would not necessarily consider themselves as bad role models. My theories about this are based on my observation of social norms. Take them on board but use the power of your own positive imagination to come up with your own theories to enlighten people.

4: MY MENTOR

Mentor is one of the most favourable words used by successful people. The environment of business entrepreneurship is a challenging sector for young people right now across the world. If you are in the midst of experienced people, and you don't have a mentor, each day will be tougher than the last. Not having a mentor is the main problem for young people in developing countries. A mentor in this context is someone who can play an advisory role for you and encourage you, particularly when you reach the climax of your efforts. That person can be your spouse, friend, co-worker, family member or anybody who is sound-minded.

Mentors are people who have genuine interest in their heart to help people. Mentors are not necessarily professional, or someone with a high degree of experience. Mentors are a role model with a physical connection to you. People are more emotionally attached to their mentor than to a role model, but the benefit gained from both is the same. Most educational institutions provide mentoring programmes for children which prepare those children to become creative and productive adults.

Sometimes school teachers are not equipped to efficiently play a mentoring role. Hence it is crucial for the government to create mentoring facilities in schools and playgrounds which will capture the imagination of children and help them to emulate one another. Initiatives might include painting the images of influential and successful people on walls in public places, writing the most powerful phrases on billboards located at community centres, inviting role models to give keynote speeches at schools, and encouraging the most intelligent children to publicly display their talents. At home introducing words like positive imagination, success, role model and mentor to children from the early stages of their lives would enhance their desire to become something incredible in the future.

How to utilise the ideas of your mentor

The secret which am about to reveal to you can't be found in other self-help books. In the last chapter I touched on how my interactions with the stories of my spiritual mentor Imam Ghazali had a profound impact on my personal spiritual journey, but I didn't reveal how I made that journey. Pay close attention to the following.

Physical interaction is really crucial for you to connect with the ideas of your mentor. It is only through that interaction you can achieve real life experience. You can also read their books and use search engines online in order to familiarise yourself with their stories.

Here is my secret: often I bought books written by Imam Ghazali and I tried my best to read each book from cover to cover at least twice. While I read, I focused thoroughly on how he approached the burning issues confronting society and how he influenced public opinion by challenging his opponents whenever he encountered them in debates. I confess I never actually saw Imam Ghazali, but his physical description which I gathered from reading his books is enough for me to use the power of my positive imagination and visualize as if I have seen him in real life.

Often while I read his books, I pretended that he was physically in front of me, passing information to me. When I gathered enough information from each book, I took three different actions.

Firstly, I would usually compare my ideas to his ideas in

order to determine which of my ideas needed improving. For example, he generated most of his ideas through pure rational thinking and the virtue of the wisdom to all his arguments are based on logic, and providing adequate evidence to support his theories.

Secondly, I focused on mirroring his personal attributes so that I could improve my weak points. For example, he is an eloquent public speaker while I am not good. He won't hesitate to engage his opponent in debates but so far I don't have the stomach to engage my opponents in debates.

Thirdly, I would forensically examine how he deals with paradoxical situations and analyses them through an intellectual lens so that I can determine the best approach on how to confront other people's theories and intellectual arguments in order to give them fair commentary.

Here is another mind blowing secret from a different dimension which will bring you a step closer to your mentor. But first look how I interact with my mentor from a different angle. I came to realise recently that I had only read just a fraction of Imam Ghazali's intellectual work, but my intention is to lay my humble hand on every single thing written by him in Arabic or English. That will be crucial to further my intellectual advancement. But although I haven't read all he wrote, because I have imagination and wild admiration about his life, amazingly I can guess what I will find in the pages of his books, without even laying my hands on them. From my past experience of his work, my imagination would reinforce my instinct as to what I am about to find. Thus I ought to guess accurately like him in the middle ages. Even though he is no longer alive, believe me from a distance he is mentoring me with his intellectual as well as spiritual guidance.

Just to give you an idea how widely he was published, according to a rough estimate he wrote well over two hundred books, which touched on almost all aspects of human affairs: with no exaggeration he is an ocean of knowledge. I often check Wikipedia to make sure I haven't missed any recent amendments to his biography and I absorb all the new information related to his academic work and the people he influenced. I have a very good feeling that one day in my meditation he will confide in me to reveal the rest of his story, so that I can share it with the world. Whenever I am confronted with a critical situation or facing a social dilemma I pause for a while by contemplating how Imam Ghazali would address that particular issue. Often I take strength from that.

Now I am going to illustrate the power of human interaction with a picture. It is common for authors to put own picture on the cover of their books. This is neither for fun nor to seek recognition for their works They are not looking for fame or trying to gain popularity to further their writing career. They use the picture to get an emotional interaction with their readers.

For example can you turn to the back cover of this book? You will see a small picture of me. If you look carefully at the picture you will notice that I wear traditional African dress, while I am smiling and looking at you. I am doing that so that while you are reading this book, I can emotionally interact with you, in order for you to make sense of what I am trying to share with you. Whenever, you lay your hand on a copy of your mentor's book use the power of your imagination and the image of your mentor to pretend that you are directly absorbing information from him in real life.

Try to engage physically with them at the first available

chance, by visiting a mentoring programme or conference where your mentor is expected to speak. Try to pay a courtesy call on them just for the sake of saying hello once in a while and learning from that. How you absorb all the information learnt through interaction with the mentor is profoundly central to your own personal advancement. In order for you to genuinely utilise such wisdom, always make sure you have three types of information: the information related to your personal attributes, the information which had inspired you to emulate someone and the information you are going to use to explore your own ideas which will subsequently help you becoming your own brand.

For an example, let use the Facebook founder Mark Zuckerberg as your mentor.

If you really want to be like him, before you begin, you must understand that simply by being a human being you already have thirty percent of his attributes. This is the fact of humanity, everybody has some of the same attributes, therefore the stage is already set for you.

Go online to familiarise yourself with the remaining seventy percent related to Mark Zuckerberg and his life, particularly how he used the power of his positive imagination to create the world class social media platform Facebook. Then combine all the information you gathered about him and divide it in to the three different sections. Don't forget that you were already thirty percent of the way there. The second thirty percent of his attributes are what you need to give yourself in order to be equal to sixty percent of him. By reaching that threshold half of your job is done.

Finally you have to learn from the remaining forty percent so that you can create your own brand. This is exactly how you can become like your mentor. However, under no circumstances copy anyone or pretend to be something which you are really not. Mentoring is all about borrowing people's ideas in order to improve your own, and not about copying them.

Let's look at it from a different angle, if you are in the position of mentoring people. The virtue of being a mentor has all the merits I discussed in relation to the role models, particularly when your mentoring involves young children. Projecting a positive image is the key to harnessing their imagination because children will then look up to you.

In 2015 while I was in the Gambia, I researched how the power of image influences people's imaginations. I approached a set of children with two D100 Gambian bank notes. One had a portrait of president Jammeh printed on the front, and the second bill had no image of him. When I asked the children who owned the D100 bill with the portrait of Jammeh, without hesitation they would respond Yaya Jammeh. When I showed them the other note D100, they would hesitate to tell me who owned the note. I tried to rephrase the question: who owns this note? Who owns the Gambian currency? Whose money is this? Amazingly their answers were the same. I reached the conclusion that portraying human images on objects is central in influencing their opinion of ownership and cultivating positive images in to their imaginations.

The value of your image alone is not sufficient to attract people's attention if you lack the utility to add value to their lives. Giving a good impression to others is the virtue everyone wants, particularly the manner which you present yourself to the public. This includes positive body language, how you conduct yourself during your interaction with people, the vocabulary you use to communicate with people, and your taste in food and clothes. Often when people offer mentoring services they don't take these things seriously, which is a mistake.

If I become a mentor, this is how I will conduct myself. First of all, I will be honest with myself by recognising that mentoring is not all about me and my life experiences, but it is also about you and what we can learn from each other. I would use the power of my positive imagination to firmly put myself in people's shoes. I will ask myself the following question: if I happened to be on the receiving end, what would I expect from these people? After determining that, I will wonder what the best method is for me to share my real life experience without showing off too much or telling vague stories just to impress people.

I won't have to show off my talent nor keep reminding people that I am special, because they will already expect that from a mentor. I will use modesty in all my language, and show respect and genuine politeness. However, I would not take myself too seriously like a courtroom judge. I would watch my behaviour and use manners and intelligence to learn from them. I will make every single interaction with me a memorable one, to allow people to further their human advancement. And I will also make sure every single conversation I hold with people who admire me is a great opportunity for them to become much better than me.

To further illustrate my point, we have to look at mentoring from a different perspective, especially for people who consider the Queen and the royal family as role models. Before we proceed with our conversation once again I will challenge you to use the power of your positive imagination to work out why you have never seen the Queen and the other prominent members of the royal family crying in public, consuming food in public, swearing in public, and apart from the balcony kiss after the royal wedding, you never see them publicly intimate with their spouses. You don't see those smoking cigarettes in public, or drinking alcohol in public, except when the Queen hosts a state banquet for foreign dignitaries.

You may recall a few years back when Prince Harry smoked cannabis, it created a big commotion in the UK and attracted negative media attention. And relatively recently on a different occasion Prince Harry was allegedly seen naked in a Los Angeles swimming pool. Again his behaviour was controversial and it attracted condemnation from the international community. You might ask yourself why, in a rage! I would put my hand on your shoulder and gently say "My friend, please calm your innocent soul, here is the reason why such behaviour always generates a public outcry." Prince Harry belongs to the most famous, powerful and important family in the world. Consequently his behaviour will influence the behaviour of millions of people around the world, and has potential to create the forces of good or evil. People do blow things out of proportion, because there is a degree of resentment towards the establishment. But whenever there are genuine grounds for constructive criticism, then it becomes an obligation for the public to express their genuine views. Usually those on the receiving end would accept public opinion in good faith. I can understand the level of pressure on institutions such as the royal family, the church and Islamic scholars, because I came from a Muslim conservative scholar's family background, which is often a target for criticism. However, most mentors are conscious of the fact that public scrutiny is always part of the package.

You can become your own super brand. Rather than being resentful towards the establishment, create your own version of a mentoring system and then become a most important person in your own right. Do not envy other people's success. There are many different ways to earn adulation without resorting to jealousy or denigration. The most effective tool for sustainable admiration is your frequent interaction with mentors, and offering people your own mentoring service so that your life will be as celebrated as the Queen and the royal family.

As I said before, in order to mentor people, physical interaction is the most effective tool, yet it is not limited to that alone. You can still inspire people with public service or inspiring stories, and even sometimes your name alone is enough to do the job for you.

For an example the Queen hardly ever engages people in conversation face to face. Millions of royal family fans never have the chance to see the Queen in real life, they just see her image on television or on rare occasions see her far in the distance. But she still inspires people through her image and title, thus they will imitate how she speaks, how she dresses, how she smiles and how she waves to people. At the first available opportunity, thousands of peoples would often put their lives on hold to queue up for hours just to see a glimpse of her.

90% of all Facebook users around the globe didn't even know who was behind Facebook but the inventor Mark Zuckerberg captured billions of people's imaginations without uttering a single word to them. By utilising his ideas in a wonderful way, millions of people can now share images from their lonely bedrooms, speak to each other without using their tongues and use their fingertips to share inspiring stories with your love ones. He created a fantasy world which presented his ideas to the public imagination and it will remain that way forever. Millions of people are using Mark Zuckerberg's inspirational method to inspire their own friends.

A few years back I reconnected with a long-time friend on Facebook for the first time in seven years. Amazingly after we had reconnected again, he became an unexpected mentor for me. When I looked at Facebook, I noticed one thing in particular about him: on his timeline were only positive images of himself and his family. Whenever he talked about something, he would only write encouraging words which can inspire people. Frequently he would post pictures he took from the gym, or important family gatherings, as well as places like university. And guess what, the most important aspect of all is that in every picture he had posited on Facebook, you could always see him smiling. As a result he had mentored me unexpectedly. Since then I adopted the same approach as his. Now whenever I am posting something on Facebook I follow his methods of communication. I cannot resist the temptation to share this experience with you guys.

Positive people displaying positive images on social media are always mentoring people without even them known it. One positive word by you in the right place has the capacity to influence the behaviour of other people. By utilising your ideas effectively, you can frequently create your own mentoring platform from other people's ideas, because no matter what people say, seeing things from a different perspective can gradually improve the world.

Next time before you go on Facebook, pause for a while, perhaps use meditation to produce something positive from the power of your imagination, and then share it with the wider world in order to mentor your own people. Even if it is just once in a while, come up with your own original idea. While you are reading this book you will notice some of my own phrases which I had invented to mentor people, such as "Feeling is more powerful than touching", and "Showing a certificate for your talent is mandatory for people who cannot display their natural talent in action" (for example the Portuguese international superstar Cristiano Ronaldo doesn't have to produce a certificate to demonstrate to the world that he can play football very well, equally I don't have to show any certificate to prove that I am a published author).

In order to increase your success rate in all your endeavours, I would like to expose you to some of my philosophical ideas: hopefully it will help you to see your own world from a different angle.

I know many intelligent people who always keep complaining "I cannot do this, I cannot do that" but often I use my own philosophy to encourage them. If you cultivate your mind, I am sure that eventually you will invent something incredible. Inventing something new might sound intimidating but in reality it is easier than you imagine.

Uttering truth is more powerful than pain you inflict on your enemies. Often you get pain from your enemy's conspiracies, and the negative impact of that is more harmful than the justice you deserve to punish them with. Therefore, whenever you utter a word, say speak the truth. Even though people might not agree with you today but eventually they will see the truth.

All human beings desire four main things in their lives: food, money, sex and power. If you want to be a good person, follow your heart, pursue your passion and help others in whatever small way you can. Big achievements are made by big effort, not by the size of your faith in God. No matter how many good qualities you have, realise that there will be moments when none of your qualities are noticed. Peace is contained in the human mind and memories but happiness is contained only in the imagination. The life of every human being is similar to an unpredictable weather pattern; nothing is guaranteed to stay the same. Living your life from moment to moment is an alternative to happiness especially for people living in the 21st century. Don't expect miracles to happen every day. Luck won't come without lucky people looking for luck. Wishful thinking is more helpful than mystical thinking, because wishful thinking will give you an incentive and the energy to strive and excel where others failed. But mystical thinking will lead you to where other people failed to excel. Honesty is the language use by good people to give comfort to society whenever it is necessarily but in reality it does not exist. And finally, being judgemental of others is the mother of all bigotry.

These are my social philosophies which are part of my daily principles and I try to live by them as well as encouraging other people to do the same.

5: FEAR IS YOUR NUMBER ONE ENEMY

Fear is an obstacle which prevents you from becoming the person you really want to be. In this final chapter I will discuss how to effectively tackle fear, including how to stamp out all the phobias which negative people bring in to your social circle. Building your emotional confidence is central to this.

Let me tell you how I conquered my own fear of flying. In late February 2013, while I was in Sydney, I called my friend who was living in Africa at that time, and I said "Hello my friend this is Yaya calling you from Sydney, Australia. How are you?" He said "Pardon me, can you repeat what you just said?" I thought he couldn't hear me properly and I repeated it. "What do you mean Australia, are you in Australia?" he asked. "How did you get there, Yaya, because all your friends know that you hate flying. So tell me, did you go by foot, or bicycle or perhaps you travelled by car to Australia?"

I laughed out loud and said I used the aeroplane to get here. I could tell from the sound of his voice that he was totally baffled, and he said "Wow Yaya finally you conquered your fear of flying and travelled from London all the way to Australia. I am really proud of you and I wish you all the best."

Now let me tell you how I did it. First it took me couple of weeks to contemplate how to challenge my phobia of long haul flights. Eventual through intense meditation and re-evaluating the world from a different perspective I have defeated my number one enemy. Finally I overcame the monumental obstacle which nearly prevented me from becoming whom I really wanted to be.

1. Through the positive power of my imagination, I came to realise that no matter how much fear I had about flying, my fear would never prevent other people from flying. But it was powerful enough to prevent me from seeing the world, and as a result I would lose every single opportunity to travel to other far off countries. Hence every day I imagined seeing other people living the type of life I dreamed of. I compared myself to people whom I most admired. And also I imagined seen myself living in a dream world where I would develop rage in my soul, jealousy towards other people's success, and envy of my contemporaries achievements in leading exactly the type of life I wanted. In such an environment anger and resentment will be on the everyday menu for me and my life would be meaningless.

2. Whether I have fear in my mind or not, it would not prevent me from answering the call of the angel of death. However, until that day I would rather carry on with my life and focus on what I am able to control while leaving the rest purely in the hands of almighty Allah.

3. If I want to fulfil all my 'me' factors in order to have a happy life, I ought to be brave and have that desire to feed my curiosity, where me and my ideas would travel far and wide and eventually conquer the world.

Although the story am about to share with you is true, I won't tell you the private details, but the story is relevant. I knew a couple from the Middle East who were dating each other for almost eight years. However, the man in question wouldn't commit to marry his partner and she was really frustrated by this. When I met her in 2015 I told her, in Muslim conservative society it is profoundly wrong to establish a sexual relationship with someone whom you don't intend to marry. I added that when the relationship becomes public there would be a social stigma attached to it which would be enough for her family to dishonour her. And I asked her why are you reluctant to ask him for marriage? Guess what? Her main barrier to asking for marriage was fear of rejection. She preferred to remain in the push and pull relationship which was totally dominated by him for the entire eight years. I try encouraging her on different occasions to push him for marriage but she didn't have the stomach to ask for it. Eventually I managed to convince her to do so.

She agreed to ask him to marry her but she would only do it when she felt that he was in a good mood for a gentle approach. However, she subsequently changed her mind. Even though she was dying inside to get married, she wouldn't ask him. She just couldn't pluck up the courage.
In the end, in order to trigger a reaction from her, this is what I said: if you ask a man to marry you and he rejects you, that is a mere rejection, but if your family finds out you are dating a man who will never marry you, you risk losing your family and the entire community will reject you, so the choice is yours.

This time my advice resonated with her so much and she did exactly as I said. But then he rejected her marriage offer straightaway and subsequently in late 2016, he dumped her by text message.

As you can imagine, she was totally devastated. At this stage I was in Africa and she rang me crying over the phone as she told me what had happened earlier that night. Equally I was devastated. Listening to her distraught voice, momentarily I was at a loss. I was trying to absorb the bad news for several minutes, yet with the shock I could not remember any comforting words to use. I blamed myself for pushing her so much, and look what happened. But in the end, I was right to do so.

Even though they were dating for almost eight years, neither his family nor hers suspected anything about their relationship. But she knew a few people who knew enough about his family background and she also knew a few friends from his inner circle to whom she could ask the right questions about him. Ever since I met her, I had my doubts about the genuineness of their relationship because in Middle Eastern culture it is totally alien and high risky for a man to date a woman for such a long time without the intention of marrying her.

But right from the beginning he had controlled their relationship. He called her whenever he wanted to, but he would only return her phone calls at his own convenience. And always whenever he had to cancel a meeting with her he would often use a text message to inform her. She became paranoid that one day perhaps he would finish their relationship by simply sending her a text message. For some reason which is only known to her, she was deeply in love with him. Thus she had disconnected from logic and rational thinking, and her fear of rejection had effectively consumed her mind.

He also offered her the 'promise of the century' which was this: his aging father was a multi- millionaire Sheik and he was the sole beneficiary of his father's fortune. However, according to him the reason why he was not interested in marrying her is that his father wouldn't allow him to marrying anyone from a western background because he did not trust Middle Eastern women who grew up in the west. But if she would only stand by him, eventually she would be entitled to receive a large chunk of that fortune which he is waiting to inherit. Tell me in this day and age who would be stupid enough to refuse such a wonderful life time miracle from the son of an Arab Sheik?

But the truth she found out about him was heart-breaking. She discovered from one of his close confidants that the man after all was bisexual, and he was a prominent member of a gay club in Sydney. Additionally he was addicted to gambling; most weekends he would visit one casino after another, and he was also living in Australia as a refugee. With such revelations she knew her Prince Charming was a professional liar. She nearly dropped dead from a heart attack. All of sudden everything began to make sense to her. How she couldn't have access to certain areas in his bedroom, and how he consumed money like a raging fire consumes petrol, as well as his unusual sexual approach towards women and how he behaved towards random men. He even used her for money; by convincing her to spent $25,000 on him and promising to pay it back, but he never did.

I told her I thought he had used and dumped you but in fact he set you free from long time modern slavery. Thank God you have your liberty after eight years of emotional captivity.

Now you know her story you can reach to your own conclusion, but you can see he had effectively used her like a toy: psychologically, emotionally and physically, while at the same time exploiting her to the maximum. Luckily, I intervened and rescued her by encouraging her to confront and conquer her fear of rejection.

The lady in question is now happily married to someone in an Islamic way, and they are now preparing to legalise their marriage in the Western way in a grand style in the near future.

We can learn a valuable lesson from this story of how fear of rejection had prevented her gaining her freedom. Fear often forces us to stay in abusive relationships which are not apparent to the outside world. Unscrupulous individuals often use fear as weapon to control people physically and emotionally.

In my example above, the man used deception to cover his tracks. Secondly, he created the fake story about his father's approval of their marriage. Thirdly, he promised her millions of dollars from a fake inheritance. And fourthly he abused her trust. From the beginning his motives were clear: he was going to use her as much as possible. She had her doubts about him, but as you know love is blind and prevented her from discovering the truth. She totally dropped her guard due to intense fear of losing a man she loved.

You can become what you want to be, but only if you are willing to confront your fear and tackle it accordingly. Occasionally fear might help people to progress in their life; however, it is essential to compare your fear against the benefit you might gain through being brave. Often you must weigh one against the other and whatever comes out on top, go along with that.

People in a relationship fear being rejected, because there is a social stigma attached to that. But fear is the emotional cancer killing couples in love. The fear of rejection of the woman in question did not prevent the man from rejecting her, but her braveness to confront that fear eventually set her free.

For example you can read hundreds of books and have access to many ideas about how to deal with society but whenever you have fear and you fail to overcome it, all your intelligence is useless. You don't necessarily have to care about other people's opinion of you and your relationship as long as you know exactly what you are doing. You will always regret your failure to overcome fear.

Certainly there will be a counter argument that a certain degree of fear is good for humanity. For example, fear of being caught prevents couples from cheating on one another: true. And fear of being caught prevents people from stealing other people's property: true. Fear of punishment prevents people from breaking the law: true. Fear of failure helps people to work harder: true. Fear of sickness encourages people to maintain a healthy life style: true. Fear of poverty encourages people to be good with their money: true. Fear of accidents causes a driver to be careful on the roads: true.

But I think it might help if I distinguish between constructive fear and negative fear. Constructive fear is a positive feeling which helps people progress in their lives. However, negative fear is the negative feeling which stops people from progressing, and it is this kind of fear which should be conquered. Anxiety from such fear would eventually lead to severe stress and depression. Negative fear will prevent you from using the power of your positive imagination which as I have told you is the key to success.

Constructive fear profoundly helps people accomplish more than people consumed by negative fear. Every human emotion has its opposite (for example love vs hate) and every human being has conflicting emotions.

For instance, men with a sexual desire for women have a good feeling, but maybe at the same time they have the negative fear of rejection, which usually prevents their approaching women. Equally women would have a genuine desire for men in order to satisfy their sexual egos but often negative fear for a damaged reputation prevents them from taking the right steps. Each individual has his or her own 'me' factors to fulfil whether by consuming food, accumulating money, craving for power and desiring sexual pleasure. But usually negative fear of failure and humiliation is predominant. Apparently just to illustrate this further, love is very powerful emotional force but hate is an equally emotional powerful negative force. Hope is a very positive feeling but despair is another powerful negative force. Feeling anxious is normal but confidence is more productive than anxiety.

Internal needs are sets of feelings circling opposite one another. External needs are the agents for those internal feelings, each of which is fighting to control you and your imagination. For example feelings of sexual desire which required both inner emotional fulfilment and external physical satisfaction would often have a conflict with the moral code. But feelings like desire for having food and drink are feelings which require fulfilment without having a conflict with moral codes.

The same attributes apply to all the following emotions; pleasure is a feeling, hope is a feeling, happens is a feeling, sadness is a feeling, anger is a feeling, envy is a feeling, pride is a feeling, greed is a feeling, humiliation is a feeling and pain is a feeling. All these feelings require fulfilment, and somehow they are connected to delivering satisfaction to the human ego.

So next time when you are confronted with fear, pause for a while and use the power of your positive imagination and visualise the positive impact against the negative impact, then immediately tackle the negative impact in order to get the best outcome. However, if the negative impact is more suitable to your circumstances, embrace the negative impact and place it in the position of positive impact. Such methods are exactly the techniques use by comedians, which is why people would often laugh at their behaviour.

Peoples in the comedy business are the most intelligent people when it comes to using information effectively to influence public opinion; they have the psychological power to trick your brain into laughing at anything which initially you wouldn't laugh at in a million years.

Here is the technique they use. Remember I stated in the previous chapter that whenever you accumulate information from whatever resource available to you make sure you divide them in to three different sections, and I had asked you to introduce two aspects of that information on yourself as well as applying the rest to be more productive. That is exactly what comedians always do. It is a very effective method.

Before an appearance, comedians do their homework to determine what the main subjects in the town are. Then they will share the information as stories, jokes, and catchphrases. Then they combine the stories and the phrases to make a really good joke. Such strategy always works. It ignites the mood of their audience and maximises the pleasure for everyone. People can see the joke relates to them so they laugh out loud. Comedians are able to do this because they have no fear or social anxiety; nothing but peace and tranquillity, therefore they can borrow your own words and use them as toys to make you laugh at your own misfortune.

If you handle information in the same way as comedians, it is beneficial for you. In pursuing our aspirations, we usually lack the skills to utilise valuable information; as a result in our journey often we find obstacles preventing us from reaching our destination. We must get quality information so that mankind will eventually liberate itself from the side effects of ignorance, and soon we will conquer the world of fear and anxiety with the knowledge of understanding human emotions. Intelligent people use their bravery with wisdom, not with pride, and they cautiously approach human challenges, not with fear but with resilience.

The power of wisdom is equivalent to the power of currencies; for example, presently UK £1 is equivalent to D61 in the Gambia, which means the value of £1 earns you much more in the Gambia than the value of D1 in the UK. Equally getting access to certain information in one country is much more valuable than other countries. On the other hand let's compare the value of Pounds Sterling against the value of gold and diamonds. If you put the weight of a £1 coin on the scales against the same weight in gold; the value for each gram of the Gold would be much higher than the coin. The same applies to diamonds. Precisely this is how the power of different wisdom carries different powers in different places.

In conclusion, I believe that knowledge is power.

Sometime last year I read on Facebook that "Knowledge comes from knowing oneself, but wisdom comes from knowing others." Is this statement true or false? You can use the power of positive imagination to work it out for yourself. However, here's what I think; getting access to more knowledge is much more advantageous for you. The purchasing power of £50 is much more powerful than the purchasing power of £5, even though both banknotes carry the same image of the Queen, they are both printed by the Bank of England and carry the same signature of the governor. But £50 is worth more than £5. I am willing to pursue more knowledge in order to improve myself as well as striving to attain more wisdom in order to share it with the wider world in my subsequent publications.

But until then, I wish that God almighty Allah will bless the readers of my books. I thank God who bestowed emotional strength in my soul and preserved physical wellbeing in my veins which helped me to complete this book.

ABOUT THE AUTHOR

My name is Alahaji' Yaya Sillah, also known as Yaya–Patchari. I was born in Jarra Sutukung Sillah Kunda in the LRR region. I am married with children. I consider my family background to be religious Muslim conservative. Initially my family belonged to the Maliki School of Islamic jurisprudence, but personally I subscribed to the Ash'ari theological school, and my spiritual mentor is Imam Ghazali. However, due to the lengthy time I spent in Western society, my views are more liberal and moderate. Professionally, I follow my Ja-hanka family Marabout tradition, which is essential for guiding people in religious matters and spiritual counselling. I obtained my early Islamic education from my grandfather Alahaji Kebba Sillah Kebba's local Majilis at Jarra Sutukung Sillah Kunda. Later on I furthered my education at Imam Baaba Camara's local Darra at Serrekunda Ebo Town.

Briefly in the late 1990s, I enrolled to study Basic English in night classes in Ebo Town and New Jeshwang, but I am largely self-educated in the language. In 2013, I undertook short courses on Creative Writing in Western Springs College in Auckland, New Zealand, and also at Al-Fridouse Islamic College in Sydney, Australia.

My area of expertise is sociology and spiritual counselling. Among my hobbies are praying, reading, writing, research, and travelling.

Cover image credit: mnsanthoshkumar / 123RF.com

www.ingramcontent.com/pod-product-compliance
Lightning Source LLC
Chambersburg PA
CBHW032048150426
43194CB00006B/451